Conversational English
American society

생활영어와
미국 사회

생활영어와 미국 사회

펴 낸 날 2025년 5월 12일

지 은 이 최영선
펴 낸 이 이기성
기획편집 이지희, 서해주, 김정훈
표지디자인 이지희
책임마케팅 강보현, 이수영
펴 낸 곳 도서출판 생각의뜰
출판등록 제 2018-000288호
주　　소 경기도 고양시 덕양구 청초로 66, 덕은리버워크 B동 1708, 1709호
전　　화 02-325-5100
팩　　스 02-325-5101
이 메 일 bookmain@think-book.com

- 책값은 표지 뒷면에 표기되어 있습니다.
  ISBN   979-11-7048-870-5(03740)

Copyright ⓒ 2025 by 최영선 All rights reserved.
· 이 책은 저작권법에 따라 보호받는 저작물이므로 무단전재와 복제를 금지합니다.
· 잘못된 책은 구입하신 곳에서 바꾸어 드립니다.

Collquail 단어들은 지난 15년간 미국 공영방송 NPR, PBS-TV, CBS TV, NBC, NY TIMES, Washington Post을 읽고 듣던 것에서 발췌. Article은 Harvard, Princeton, Yale, Stanford의 글이며 미국의 경제와 정치의 문제점을 지적한 글을 reading materials로 사용하였습니다. Definition은 사전 Webster- Merriam을 사용하였습니다.

최영선 지음

Conversational English
American society

생활영어와
미국 사회

생각의 뜰

Preface 머리말

생활영어와
미국 사회

✏ 시골, 벽지에 사는 학생, 외국 지사원, 유학생, 이민자들에게 도움될 영어, 생활 정보와 미국의 학교, 학군선택의 정보를 찾아 작성했습니다.

내가 가르치던 곳의 마을버스는 두 시간 만에 다녀서 학생들이 우리 집에 공부 배우러 오지 못하였고, 읍내 도서관에는 공부할 영어책이 마땅치 않아 미국학교에서 선택한 책을 복사하여 썼습니다. 2023년, 학교에 학생 수가 60명이 못 되는 학교가 1,300 학교가 넘는다는 연합뉴스 보도가 있었습니다. 다행히도 3대째 우리 집에서 읽어주고 있는 아동 책을 무료로 듣고, 보고 읽을 좋은 책들을 YouTube가 인터넷에 올려 놓았습니다.

영어 선생님이 부족한 시골, 교육시설이 부족한 섬 학교에 좋은 책을 보내 무료로 보고, 읽고, 듣고 서울처럼 공부할수 있으면 하는 바람입니다. 미국 아동, 청소년 수상작 수여하는 Caldicott, Newberry, Horn Book, ALA의 명작, 인기있는 작가 Judy Bloom, B.Clearly, 두 번 상 받은 K. Paterson의 좋은 책들은 미국 전역 학군, 도서관에서 추천한 책들입니다.

Contents

Preface 머리말   5

Chapter 1.	교육 I	8
Chapter 2.	교육 II	16
Chapter 3.	소비자	25
Chapter 4.	쇼핑	30
Chapter 5.	패션	38
Chapter 6.	데이트 & 결혼	45
Chapter 7.	식당	51
Chapter 8.	나이트 클럽	60
Chapter 9.	파티	69
Chapter 10.	스포츠	75
Chapter 11-1.	여행	84
Chapter 11-2.	여행(교통)	93
Chapter 12.	전화	99
Chapter 13.	건강 & 의학	102

Chapter 14.	인종차별 & 계급사회	109
Chapter 15.	공 해	113
Chapter 16.	종 교	118
Chapter 17-1.	언론 TV & 예술	124
Chapter 17-2.	연예 & TV	128
Chapter 17-3.	예 술	134
Chapter 17-4.	종합 예술	140
Chapter 18-1.	경제 + ESOP	143
Chapter 18-2.	한국 경제	150
Chapter 18-3.	기업 운영	152
Chapter 18-4.	금융 & 임금격차	160
Chapter 18-5.	경 영	167
Chapter 19.	직장 & 노조	183
Chapter 20-1.	정치 – 정부	191
Chapter 20-2.	정치 – 입법부	200
Chapter 20-3.	정치 – 사법부	209
Chapter 21.	아랍국가의 독재자 후세인	216

부 록   218

Chapter 1.

교육

서민학생, 시골학생 지원정책
(Affirmative Action)

생활영어 교육 1-1

1. Her parents kept her naughty friends at arm's length from their daughter.
   딸의 부모는 딸을 나쁜 친구들과 거리를 두게 하였다.
   ** Keep distance from something or somebody.

2. Some poor kids fell through the cracks when a family goes through a tough time.
   가난한 아이들은 집안이 힘들 때 아이들을 소홀히 하였다.
   ** To be neglected.

3. The girl, a 5th grader, wet behind the ears, loves to put on long artificial eyelashes.
   이마에 피도 마르지 않은 5학년 초등학교 여학생이 긴 속눈썹 달기를 좋아한다.
   ** Immature.

4. The boy is a chip off the old block. Look at the boy laughing.
   그 남자 아이는 자기 아버지를 빼다 박았다. 웃는 아이를 보게!
   ** A person who closely resembles a parent.

5. The apple doesn't fall far from the tree. His dad was a great writer.
   자식들은 부모의 자질(gene)을 가지고 태어난다는 뜻.
   작가인 아버지의 자질이 있다.
   ** A child usually has a similar character or similar qualities to his or her parents.

6. Her mom should not raise her daughter to be a Cinderella syndrome.
   그녀의 어머니는 딸에게 공주병을 심어주지 말아야 한다. [독립성보다는 의지하며 멋진 왕자를 기다리는 형]
   **Cinderella syndrome is defined as a fear of independence With an unconscious desire to be taken care of by others

7. The school tried to nip the student smoking in the bud.
   그 학교는 담배 피우는 학생의 버릇을 일찍 중지시키려 하였다.
   **To put an end to something before it develops into something larger.

8. He turned over a new leaf since he returned to school from suspension.
   그는 정학 후 학교에 돌아와 새 사람이 되었다.
   ** To stop old, bad habits and start a fresh start.

9. His mom talks his ear off whenever he gets a bad report card.
   성적표가 나쁘면 그의 어머니 잔소리에 귀가 따갑다.
   ** To bore someone with too much talk.

10. The teacher said it over and over, but it goes in the one ear and out the other.
    선생님은 말을 하고 또 해도, 그아이 한 귀로 들어가면 다른 귀로 나가버린다.

생활영어 교육 1-2

1. He was spending a lot of time at the library, so we put two and two together and realized that he was going to take the SAT.
   그는 도서관에서 많은 시간을 보냈다. 그래서 우리는 그가 수능시험을 치는 것을 알아차렸다.
   ** To guess the truth about a situation.

2. His mom should put her foot down when the kid misbehaves.
   아이 행실이 나쁘면 어머니는 아이들에게 단호하게 해야 한다.
   ** To take a firm position.

3. His dad can't stand his son hanging out with the wrong crowd.
   그 아이 아버지는 아이가 잘못된 무리와 어울려 다니는 걸 견디지 못한다.
   ** To spend much of one's time; frequent a place.

4. His dad threw up his hands when his boy was suspended for fist fight.
   그 아이가 싸움 때문에 정학을 받자 아버지는 두 손 들었다.
   ** To show that you are shocked. [기권]

5. Her daughter sheds dramatic <u>crocodile tears</u> when she lost her wallet in front of family.

   그녀의 딸은 지갑을 잃어버릴 때는 식구들 앞에서 거짓으로 운다.

   ** Insincere crying, false or affected tears.

6. His classmates used to <u>lay hands on</u> small kids.

   그 반 학생은 체구가 작은 학생들에게 손찌검을 했었다.

   ** 1. To attack, injure, or punish physically.
   ** 2. To touch or grasp someone, often with the threat of violence.

7. "Liar, Liar, pants on fire!"

   거짓말 하다 들킨 아이를 놀리는 문장('얼레꼴레리'와 유사)

   ** often used to accuse someone of lying.

8. Why did you <u>rat on</u> me to our teacher when I broke the widow?

   내가 창문을 부쉈을때 왜 너는 우리 선생님에게 나를 고자질했니?

   ** To inform an authority figure of one's bad or illegal behavior.

9. The kid <u>talked</u> our girl <u>into</u> skipping the school again.

   그 아이가 우리집 딸을 설득시켜 또 학교를 결석했다.

   ** To persuade someone to do something.

10. The kid <u>took it out on</u> his mom when his big brother asked him to do an errand.

    형이 동생에게 심부름을 시켰더니 동생은 어머니에게 화풀이를 하였다.

    [어머니가 형에게 시킨 일을 형이 동생에게 시킬 때]

    **To punish or harm someone or something because one is angry or disturbed about something.

11. <u>Corporal punishment</u> gives kids negative influence such a aggressive behavior.

    체벌은 아이들에게 거칠어지는 행동과 같은 부정적인 영향을 준다.

    ** Physical punishment, as flogging, inflicted on the body of one convicted of wrong doings.

12. The kid couldn't stand his dad's nagging.
    그 아이는 아버지의 잔소리를 견딜 수 없었다.
    ** To annoy by persistent fault finding, complaints, or demands.

13. The 50 million kids skipped school because they have been constantly bullied at school in 2015 in the USA.
    2015년 미국에서 5천만명의 아이들은 (나쁜 학생에게) 괴롭힘을 당하여 학교를 결석하였다.
    ** Habitually seeks to harm or intimidate those whom they perceive themselves as vulnerable.

14. Angry dad grounded his boy for two weeks after the Police arrested him for smoking.
    담배 피우다 아들이 경찰에게 체포당해 화난 아버지가 2주간 벌을 주었다.
    ** To punish a kid for misbehavior.

15. The kid was beaten up for calling names to them.
    그 아이는 그들에게 모욕적인 말을 하다가 두들겨 맞았다.
    **To insult someone. [나쁜놈, 사기꾼 같은 표현]

🔍 미국교육 정보… 힘들어지는 교육 현실(Reverse Affirmative Action)

　　개천에서 용 난다는 말이 한국에서 사라지듯, 미국에서도 사라지는 현상입니다. 우리 메이슨(Mason) 유치원 등록금이 2023년 $36,000이었다(West LA 지역). 동부 보스턴 주의 명문대학 가려는 고등학생들 사립고등학교(prep schools) 등록금과 기숙사비가 $60,000~ $70,000이며, 명문대학 등록금도 1년에 $6만~$7만이다.
　　소수민족, 유색인종의 대부분 자식들은 교육시설이나 좋은 선생님 찾기가 힘든 시골, 가난한 학군에서 교육을 받아서 대체로 수능시험 평균점수가 1,030점 근처이다. 그런데 명문대가 받는 학생들은 1,450점을 넘어야 한다.
　　그래서 서민들의 교육 평등이 오래 전부터 문제점으로 나타나고 있다.

🔍 저소득층 지원정책(Affermative Action)

미국 존슨(Johnson) 대통령은 소수민족에게도 공정하게 기회를 주자고 1962년 정책을 발표하였다. 그 이후 우체국 직원부터 유색인종인 한국 이민자들이 직장을 많이 잡게 되고 명문대학에 흑인 대학생들도 입학률이 9%에서 15%로 증가하였다. 저소득층인 흑인, 히스페닉(Hispanic), 아랍, 동양인 자식들의 명문대학 입학률이 높아졌다. 이를 반대하는 사람들은 이 정책이 백인이나 성적이 좋은 학생을 차별(reverse discrimination)하는 제도라고 하여 2023년 백인 공화당 대법관이 많은 대법원은 6:3으로 저소득층의 유색인종 지원 혜택을 중지시켰다. 2025년 다시 대통령 당선된 트럼프역시 이 지원제도를 중지시켰다.

Affirmative action programs – including targeted outreach and recruitment efforts, the use of non-traditional criteria for hiring and admissions, after-school and mentorship programs, and training and apprenticeship opportunities are tailored to fit specific instances where race and gender must be taken into account in order to provide fair and equal access to minorities, Americans, and women. These programs recognize and strive to correct the barriers that continue to block the paths of many individual Including women, Native Americans, Arab Americans, Latinos, Asian Americans, and African Americans.

⟨By ACLU⟩

🔍 대학 등록금 & 기숙사비(Calf. & East Coast)

서민가족 학생들이 비싼 명문대학 입학을 돕기 위한 지원 정책을 만들었다. 대부분 부자집들은 명문대학에 가려고 명문 사립고등학교가 (prep school) 있는 부자 동네에 살고 있다. 사립고 대입 준비(Prep 고교) 등록금은 $50,000, $60,000이 넘는다. 그래서 서민을 위한 제도로 무료 공립학교에 특별고교(magnet, IB 학교)를 세웠다(아래 교육단어 참조). 부지런한 학생들은 명문대학에 가려고 그런 학교를 찾아 입학을 한다. 그래도 대학입시 준비하는 사립학교(prep)보다 수능시험 성적이 떨어져 종교단체가 등록금을 저렴하게 받는 미션-학교(Parochial school) 가는 학생들이 꽤 많이 있다.

2018년 미국 고등학생 수능시험 평균 성적은 1,023점인데, 명문 사립대학 가려면 1,500점 이상이 되어야 한다. 명문대 졸업생들의 초급 봉급은 평균 $80,000이다.

🔍 학교나 교육계에서 자주 사용하는 단어

1. SAT: 수능시험(Scholastic Assessment Test) 1,600점 만점(수학 800점, 영어 800점)
2. PSAT: 예비 수능시험
3. ACT(American College Test): 수능시험의 일종. 36점 만점
4. AP(advanced placement): 대학에서 택하는 과목을 고등학교에서 미리 택하는 과목. 대학을 일찍 졸업하려고.
5. Parochial school : 사립 중·고등학교(한국에서 말하는 미션스쿨). 등록금이 있고 수준 낮은 공립 고등학교를 가지 않으려고.
6. Prep school: 등록금이 비싼 사립 중·고등학교, 명문대학을 목표로 공부 가르치는 학교(preparatory school)
7. magnet school: 공립학교가 좋지 않은 지역에서 성적이 좋은 학생을 선발하여 교육시키는 공립학교(gifted student 위한 프로그램)
8. charter school: 정부의 돈으로 만든 독립적인 학교. 지방정부의 운영 잘못으로(bureaucratic huddle) 공립학교 조직에서 벗어나 독립적으로 설립한 학교. It is a public school of choice that operates with more autonomy and accountability than traditional public schools.
9. GED(General Educational Development) 고등학교 졸업장 없는 학생들이 시험을 보아 고졸 실력을 시험으로 받는 자격증. 대학에서 요구하는 곳이 있음.
10. Boarding School: 기숙사 생활하는 학교(room & board)
11. IB school: 성적이 좋은 학생을 모아 가르치는 무료 공립학교, 미국은 공립학교 옆에 병설학교로 만들었음. 스위스에서 만든 학교로 세계 140국가들이 이 학교 프로그램(Curriculum)을 같이 가르친다.
One of the most well-known and longest-running. Systems of international education is the International Baccalaureate (IB) curriculum. Founded in 1968 in Switzerland, the IB programme is now taught at more than 3,000 schools across more than 140 countries worldwide.

🔍 고소득층 학군: SAT 성적 & 등록금

1. 케네디컷(Connecticut) 주
   - Choate Rosemary Hall: 평균 수능시험 성적: 1,430. 등록금- $67,380. 졸업생- John F. Kennedy
   - The Hotchkiss–Lakeville 학교. SAT 점수: 1,470. $72,620 with 기숙사비.

2. 메사추세츠(Massachusetts) 주
   - Groton High, 등록금+기숙사비, SAT: 1,460. $59,995. 졸업생: Roosevelt 대통령, J P Morgan.
   - Phillips Academy Andover. SAT 평균: 1,446점. $69,000. 졸업생: 부시(Bush) 두 대통령

3. 캘리포니아(California) 주
   - The Nueva Middle @ San Mateo. SAT: 1,506. $49,990.
   - The College Prep.@Oakland. SAT 1,513. $55,980.
   .The Webb: ...Claremont, calf... SAT 1,505. $76,985

   ***　　***　　***

   노벨수상자 논문을 공부하려면 영어를 읽어야 합니다.
   영어권 노벨상: 575명 논문(미국: 411, 영국: 137, 카나다: 27).
   타국 언어 수상자: 319명 논문(독일: 115, 불란서: 75, 일본: 29).

Chapter 2.

교육 II

학군, 주립대학
(School district, State university)

생활영어 교육 2-1

1. The trouble maker <u>plays hooky</u> for the fun of it.
   그 말썽꾸러기는 재미로 (학교를) 땡땡이친다.
   ** To deliberately avoid going to school

2. The principal <u>threw a book at</u> the kid who vandalized the Gym. equipment.
   교장 선생님은 운동기구를 부순 소년을 심히 처벌하였다.
   ** To punish severely.

3. The boy <u>cribbed</u> the answer from his classmate.
   그 소년은 자기 반 학생에게서 답을 커닝하였다.
   ** cunning: sly, 간교한 뜻. Crib: 훔쳐보다.

4. His teacher <u>called the boy on the carpet</u> for the graffiti on the wall.
   선생이 벽 낙서한 그 아이를 심히 책망하였다.
   ** To reprimand, strong official criticism.

5. The student will have a double major to have something to <u>fall back on</u>.
   그 학생은 만일을 위해 전공을 두 개 할 것이다.
   ** To rely on.

생활영어 교육 2-2

1. Even the lazy boy <u>crams</u> for the finals.
   그 게으른 소년도 기말고사에 벼락공부를 한다.
   ** Study intensely over a short period of time just before an examination.

2. The physics test will have problems that will <u>go over the kids heads</u>.
   학생들이 이해하기 힘든 문제가 물리 시험문제에 나올 것이다.
   ** Too difficult to understand.

3. The boy was suspended for 2 weeks because of the graffiti.
   벽 낙서로 그 아이는 2주 정학을 받았다.
   ** Words or drawings, especially humorous, rude, or political, on walls, doors, etc. in public.
   Suspend: Stop something from being active, either temporarily.

4. Tardiness is simply caused by a lack of respect for class start times.
   지각은 간단히 말하면 수업시작 시간을 무시하는 원인이다.

5. The boy will repeat 11th grade for bullying other kids.
   그 학생은 다른 학생들을 괴롭혀서 고2를 재수를 할 것이다.
   ** Repeat: 재수. Bully: to intimidate or hurt.

6. His classmate takes a crash course for the SAT.
   그의 반학생들은 수능시험을 보려 단기 속성반을 택한다.
   ** A rapid & intense class to study.

7. Some of his friends take AP classes for a head start.
   그의 일부 친구들은 미리 배우려고 AP 과목(대학 과목)을 택한다.
   ** An advantage given in any competition.

8. The teacher won't let the student's cheating slide.
   그 선생은 그가 커닝한 것을 슬쩍 넘어가지 않을 것이다.
   ** To overlook.

9. The student is beating his brain out to finish the research paper.
   그 학생은 연구논문을 끝마치려 머리를 싸매고 있다.
   **Try hard.

10. The kid learned a lesson the hard way by the expulsion.
    그 아이는 퇴학을 당하고 힘들게 고통을 배웠다.
    ** To learn something by experience, especially by an unpleasant experience.
    **[작은 실수 하나로 심한 희생을 당해 큰 교훈을 받았다.]

11. His mom can not handle her kid's temper tantrum.
    그 아이 엄마는 그 아이 생떼를 다룰 수 없다.
    ** brief episodes of extreme, unpleasant, and sometimes aggressive behaviors in response to frustration or anger.

Find an unfit word

A. Don't _____ up the test.
   ① blow ② crush ③ goof ④ mess ⑤ screw

B. He will repeat again if he _____ school.
   ① cuts ② ditches ③ dodges ④ skips

*** Answer: A-②, B-③

🔍 학군 정보와 저렴한 주립대학

명문 사립대학은 동부에 많고, 명문 주립대학은 캘리포니아 주에 많다. 주립대학 등록금은 그 주에 사는 학생들에게는 아주 저렴하다. 대부분 명문대학의 수능시험 점수는 1,500 이상이어야 입학 가능성이 높다. 그 캐리훠니아에 거주하는 학생들은 주립대학 등록금이 저렴하지만, 반면 집값이 높은 지역이 많다.
 - 주립대학 일년 등록금: $13,000~$21,000
 - 주립대학-타주학생: $50,000~$65,000
 - 사립 명문대학 등록금: $53,000~$76,000 +기숙사비
   *** 기숙사비: $15,000~18,000(2022~23년)
이런 문제 때문에 일반 서민들에게 거주지가 중요하다.

🔍 50개 명문 미국 주립대학 by CBS-TV in 2023

사립대학은 $60,000~80,000이지만 상당수의 주립대학들은 대부분 $20,000 미만이다.

🔍 좋은 주립 대학교 이름, 주소, 일년 등록금, 입학 성적

UCLA, Los Angeles. California: $16,476. SAT 1,560.
Michigan in Ann Arbor Michigan: $17,832. SAT: 1,360.
Univ. of Calif. In Berkeley, Calf.: $19,200. SAT .1,530.
Georgia Institute of Tech. Atlanta: $17,410. SAT. 1,460.
Univ. of Virginia. Charlottesville: $19,043. SAT: 1,540.

* 나머지 50개 명문 주립대학 등록금, SAT 입학점수 부록-1에 있음

미국 내 다른 교육제도

A. 초급대학(Community College or Junior College)
B. 홈-스쿨(home schoolling)
C. 온라인 학교(On-Line school)
D. 유아, 영어책 추천

2-3A: 초급대학(Community or Junior College,or City College)

2년제 초급대학은 기술과 기초교육을 받고 자격증(Licence)을 받거나 초급대학에서 받은 학점을 인정해 주는 4년제 대학으로 전학한다. 정규대학애서 학점을 인정하는 초급대학을 선택하여야 4년제 대학 졸업장(bachror degree)을 받을 때 등록금과 시간 절약이 됨.
미국 학생들은 4년제 대학 등록금이 비싸 초급대학에서 저렴한 등록금으로 학점을 모아 받은 학점을 가지고 4년제 대학으로 전학하는 학생들이 많다. 일부는 레디에션-태러피(Radiation therapy) 보조간호사(nursing aid), 보험사, 부동산직원(real estate agent), 미용사 자격증을 받는다.
고졸 졸업장이나 고졸자격 합격증(GED)을 요구하는 학교도 있다.
A community college, sometimes known as a junior college is a higher Education institution that provides a two-year curriculum that can provide certificates, diplomas, and associate degrees. Community college degree programs typically take around two years to complete, but certification programs can take significantly less time.
AOL Jobs estimates some certificate programs range in length from months to one year. In addition, coursework for these types of programs is often offered in the evenings or on weekends for students.

Certifications (communitycollegereview.com)
How To Transfer From Community College To University: A Guide

WEB Apr 3, 2024 · Community colleges provide an excellent option for higher education students seeking affordability and flexibility. Community colleges typically focus on two-year associate degrees and certificates...
사립 기술대학들은 졸업해도 취직이 잘되지 않는 학교들도 있는데, 등록금으로 돈 버는 학교들이 있으니 많은 주의를 요한다.
대통령 트럼프도 부동산 대학교를 2005년에 세우고 학생들에게 $19,000부터 $35,000 등록금을 받고 교육의 질이 낮은 학과나 교육과정(Work shop, seminars etc)을 가르치다가 고소당하고 $25,000,000벌금을 냈다.

초급대학 일년 등록금

1. 로스 안제레스 지역(Los Angeles):일년에 $3,305.
   타주 학생: $4,900~ 5,400.
2. 시카고 지역(Chicago area): 일년에 $4,380.
3. 뉴욕시 지역: $3,100 ~ 5,600.

홈스쿨링(Home schooling)

반 학생들에게 괴롭힘당하는 소녀, 소년들, 신체 장애 있는 청소년을 위한 좋은 교육방법의 일종이다. 미국의 한 언론사에 의하면 5천만명의 학생들이 괴로움 때문에 학교를 결석한다는 보도가 있었다. 미국의 한 홈-스쿨은 10만명이 넘는 멤버가 있다.
알래스카에 사는 한 선생님은 겨울에 제설작업 문제 때문에 헬리콥터로 작은마을에서 하룻밤 머무르며 숙제를 주고받고, 또 헬리콥터를 타고 다른 마을로 이동하는 선생님도 만나 보았다.
한국이나 미국에 명문대 엘리트 학생 5% 이야기만 자주 듣는데, 70% 차지하는 학생들 위한 제도도 많이 필요하다. 집에서 부모가 가르치거나 인터넷을 통한 온라인 학교의 질을 높여 한국의 시골 힉생들이 한국의 유용한 시민이 많이 되기를.

홈스쿨 장단점, 미국 공영 방송국- NPR

어떤 부모는 홈스쿨을 무척 좋아한다고 말함.
Parents On The Pros And Cons Of Homeschooling: NPR
Advantages of Homeschooling - FamilyEducation
As Many Parents Fret Over Remote Learning, Some Find Their Kids Are Thriving.

온라인 학교(On-Line School)

학생수가 작은 학교, 섬, 시골의 문제점을 해결하는 장점.
Some Children With ADHD And Autism Thrive In Online School Over In-Person : NPR

🔍 좋은 온라인 대학교

U.S. News evaluated several factors to rank the best online bachelor's degree programs, including graduation rates, faculty credentials and services available remotely.

🔍 The Best Accredited Online Colleges of 2024 - US News

Colleges are ranked based on their graduation rate, Quality of education. The school reputation, cost, and the expectation and give you the best chance to succeed. There are many colleges that make the worst colleges in America list either because they have a ridiculously high drop-out rate, are way too expensive, are in the middle of lawsuits, or just have a rotten reputation.

🔍 50개 자격미달 대학교. 제공 언론사-MSN

The 50 Worst Colleges In America Ranked (msn.com)

조기 교육: 유아~초등학생 추천하는 무료 교재

미국 아동, 청소년 수상작 Caldicott, Newberry, Horn Book, ALA의 수상작, 인기있는 작가 Judy Bloom, B. Clearly, 두번 상 받은 K. Paterson의 좋은 책들을 도서관, 학교에 전해 줍시다.
YouTube에서 무료로 볼 수 있으며, 듣고 글도 읽을 수 있음.

🔍 유아: 우리 집에서 3대째 읽어주고 있는 classic 명단

1. **Are you my Mother? 〈by PD Eastman〉 5분 16초.**
   Are You My Mother? By P.D. Eastman Read Aloud (youtube.com)
2. **Harry the Dirty Dog. 〈by G. Zion〉 4분 6초**
   HARRY the Dirty Dog – Read Aloud Funny Stories (youtube.com)
3. **The Hungry Caterpillar 〈E. Carle〉 4분 30초.**
   The Very Hungry Caterpillar by Eric Carle Read Aloud (youtube.com)
4. **The Three Little Pigs 5분.**
   The Three Little Pigs – Read aloud in fullscreen with music and sound effects! (youtube.com)
5. **Ms. Nelson is missing. 〈H. Allard & J. Marshall.〉 5분.**
   Miss Nelson Is Missing – Book Read Aloud (youtube.com)
6. **Martha Speaks. 〈by S. Meddaugh〉 10분.**
   MARTHA SPEAKS by Susan Meddaugh : Kids Books Read Aloud (youtube.com)
7. **Curious George 〈By H.A. Rey〉 7분 33초.**
   THE ORIGINAL CURIOUS GEORGE by H.A. Rey – Books for Children Read Aloud! (youtube.com)

Silly한데 유아들은 흥미있는 모양, 인기가 많아 TV연재로 나왔으니 원본 책을 찾읍시다. PBS TV에 "Thomas & Friend"는 2021년까지 584개의 이야기가 연재로 나왔습니다. 우리 집 Alex는 2살경부터 하루에 2시간 정도 봄. 문장이 없는 단점이 있다.
*** 만화 영화는 부모들이 영어로 말하지 않는 유아에게 영어를 가르치는 최고의 교재입니다.

Mark는 영어 못하는 할머니라 Thomas & Friends, 소라는 Finding Nemo와 Monster Inc.을 그만 보라고 해도 더 보겠다고 애원한다. 대화를 잘못 알아들어도 그림으로 이야기를 눈치껏 알아 들으며 영어를 배운다.
*** 초등학교 3학년 이상, 중·고 교재는 부록-2에 있습니다.

🔍 교재 선택을 위해 비교할 단어 Sample

아동 언어 -- 수능시험단어 -- colloquial, slang.
실수 -- boo-boo -- blunder, injury -- XXXX
아픔 -- ouch -- affliction. -- XXXX
상처 -- owie -- injury, pain -- XXXX
엉덩이. behind -- buttock -- ass, butt, fanny. rear end.
멍청이 -- dumb -- Imbecile -- knucklehead, numb suckle, meat head.
폭발하다 -- snap -- freak out (outburst)
징그러운 -- Yucky -- disgusting -- gross.
소변보다 -- pee -- urinate -- piss, take a leak.
잡담하다 -- chat -- prattle -- shoot the breeze, chew the fat.
비위마추다 -- flatter -- kiss one's butt, brown nose.
작살내다 -- crush -- devastate -- kick one's ass.

🔍 불우한 어린 청소년 도움 주는 배우 Paul Newman

심히 아픈 청소년, 생을 마감할 청소년들을 위해 캠핑장에 와서 식구들과 함께 즐겁게 지내게 하려고 30여개 캠핑장을 만들었다.

More than 30 years ago, Paul Newman started a free where kids could escape the fear and isolation of their medical conditions and, in his words,"raise a little hell." This remarkable concept sparked a quiet movement, and that one camp launched a global network. Today, there are 30 camps and programs serving the needs of children. The mission was to create opportunities for children with serious illnesses and their families to reach beyond illness and discover joy,…

Chapter 3.

소비깡

Consumerism &
Payday Loan

1. You can return any merchandise to most department stores to give a break to compulsive buyers.
   대부분 백화점에서는 충동적으로 물건을 구입하는 구매자를 도우려고 구매자가 매입한 상품을 이유 없이 반품을 받습니다.
   ** Buyer with obsessively uncontrollable buying habit.

2. Many skin care products put ads with unsubstantiated claims.
   많은 피부 관리 상품들은 입증 안 된 주장을 광고합니다.
   ** Not supported or proven by evidence.

3. Some car repair shops demanded outrageously inflated prices.
   일부 자동차 수리점은 부풀린 청구서로 엄청나게 돈을 요구하였다.
   ** Excessively or unreasonably high.

4. Dana, a phony German heiress, defrauded banks and an airplane leasing owner.
   자기가 독일 부잣집 상속자라고 속인 Dana는 은행들과 비행기 임대업자를 횡령하였다.
   ** Illegally obtain money from by deception:

5. Parents of a kid, who'd never played soccer, paid $1.2 million to a soccer coach to make the girl as a star soccer player to get into an Ivy League college.
   축구를 해보지도 않은 아이를 일류 축구선수로 만들어 명문대로 입학시키려고 그 소녀의 부모가 축구 코치에게 $120만 불을 지불하였다.

6. A newspaper reported on the second cheating of W.F. Bank's Chairman with customers' deposits. It drove the final nail in his coffin.
   그 신문은 두 번 째 고객의 돈을 횡령한 WF은행 회장 사 건을 보도하였다. 그 횡령은 그 회장이 스스로 자기를 파멸시킨 최후의 타격이었다.
   ** To perform some destructive(or self-destructive) act

7. A vaccine for HIV has become something of a scientific holy grail.
   HIV 백신은 과학문명이 추구하던 귀중한 명품이 되었다.
   ** Any desired ambition or goal, unobtainable. ultimate goal.

예수님이 마지막 식사 때 마신 잔

8. The customer requested a new laptop because the clerk's excuse just didn't hold water.
   그 직원의 변명은 진실이 아니라 손님은 새 컴퓨터를 요구하였다.
   ** To seem to be true or reasonable.

9. We were up to our neck in workload last month.
   우리는 지난달에 일감이 무척 쌓였다.
   ** (일거리나 짜증, 분노가) 무척 쌓인.

10. P. drug firm tried white wash the addictiveness to avoid $8 billion settlement.
    P 제약회사는 80억 불(벌금)을 내지 않으려 자기들이 생산한 약의 중독성의 사실을 숨기려 하였다.
    ** Deliberately attempt to conceal unpleasant facts.

11. Déjà vu: A train derailment 40 years ago holds clues for the Ohio city's future in 2023.
    2023년 오하이오 기차 탈선은 40년 전 기차 탈선을 연상시키는 데자뷔 같았다.
    ** A feeling of having already seen or experienced.
    전에 듣거나 보지 못한 장소나 음악이 전에 보거나 들은 것처럼 느껴지는 것.

12. US SEC charged investment adviser GPB Capital Holdings and three executives defrauding over 17,000 retail investors in a Ponzi-scheme. [피라밋 같은 사기 종류]
    판지(Ponzi) 같은 사기로 투자회사 GPB와 간부 3명이 17천 명의 투자가들을 횡령했다고 정부기관(SEC)이 주장하였다.
    ** An investment fraud that pays existing investors with funds collected from new investors.

🔍 급여 대출(Pay Day Loan)

급히 현금이 필요한 서민들은 가게 'PAY-Day Loan'에 찾아간다. 이자는 평균 12%인데 빌린 돈을 제시간에 지불 못하면 처음 계약이 무산된다(nullified).

새로운 이자율은 400%로 올린다. 그들이 빌리는 금액은 대부분 $350~$500이며, 수표를 미리 써주고(pre dated) 돈을 빌린다. 미국 내에 20,000여 개가 있다.

If the loan cannot be paid back in full at the end of the term, it has to be renewed, extended, or another loan taken out to cover the first loan. Fees are charged for each transaction the annual percentage rates on payday loans are extremely high, around 400% or higher. Lenders ask that borrowers agree to pre-authorized electronic withdrawals from a bank account, then withdrawals that do cover the full payment or that cover interest while leaving principal untouched.

By New York State Government

🔍 소비자 보호국 & 연방거래 위원회

2020년 소비자 보호국의 자료에서 미국 내 기업들 중 10개의 분야에 소비자들이 280,000여 건의 불만을 신고하였다.

🔍 FDC-Federal Trade Commision

As the nation's consumer protection agency, the reports about scammers that cheat people out of money and businesses that don't make good on their promises. We share these reports with our law enforcement partners and use them to investigate fraud and eliminate unfair business practices. Each year, the FTC also releases a report with information about the number and of reports we receive.

Bureau of Consumer Protection | Federal Trade Commission (ftc.gov)

🔍 소비자 보호국(Bureau of Consumer Protection)

⟨Top10 Consumer Complaints in 2020⟩

2020년 소비자 280,413건.

1. 자동차 매입과 수리(Sales & Repair)
2. 집수리(Home Improvement)
3. 소매상 매입
4. 고리대금업(Predatory Lending)
5. 집주인과 임대의 분쟁(Landlord/Tenant Dispute)
6. 유선인터넷 사용료 조작(Cable Billing, Price Gausing)
7. 시에서 발행하는 고지서(Utility Bill: 전기, 수도, 도시가스)
8. 거짓 광고(False Advertising)
9. 여행사
10. 인터넷 방송 판매(Internet Sales)

Nation's Top 10 Consumer Complaints · Consumer Federation of Ameri

🔍 Voice Phishing(전화로 타인의 정보를 이용하여 돈을 갈취하는 수법)

Voice phishing is a type of scam where fraudsters use phone calls and voice messages to steal personal information or money from their victims.

🔍 타이틀 회사(Title Company)

집이나 건물, 대지를 사고 팔 때 제3자로 이 회사가 건물의 새 소유자를 등록시켜주고 전 소유자의 담보나 빚을 찾아 판매가격에 적용하여 판매를 법적으로 정리해주는 기업. 비용은 판매액의 0.5%나 융자액(loan의) 0.5%.

소비자 보호국(Consumer Affairs)

When you buy a piece of real estate, a title company makes sure the seller has a legal right to sell the property and that the buyer isn't purchasing a home with outstanding taxes or mortgages on it. In other words, the title company is responsible for the legality of a real estate purchase.

https://www.consumeraffairs.com/finance/what-does-a-title-company-do.html

Chapter 4.
쇼 핑

Shopping

생활영어 쇼핑 1-1

1. The watches are flying off the shelves. Get it now.
   그 시계는 불티나게 팔린다니 지금 사세요.
   ** To sell very quickly.

2. The food prices go through the roof during the lunar new year.
   설날 때 식품가격이 천정부지로 오른다.
   **To rise to a very high level.

3. The used car salesman lied through his teeth.
   중고차 판매원은 입에 침도 바르지 않고 거짓말하였다.
   ** To say something completely false.

4. The auction house hired a few shills to maximize their profits.
   경매장은 수익을 최고로 올리려고 몇 명의 바람잡이를 고용했다.
   ** An accomplice of a hawker, gambler, or swindler.

5. He was duped by a fly by night repair man.
   그는 사기꾼 수리공에게 사기를 당했다.
   ** Untrustworthy in business.

6. He bought the house for a song from an old lady.
   그는 노인에게서 그 집을 저렴하게 매입했다.
   ** Very cheaply.

7. The street vendor tried to pass off a synthetic diamond as a genuine diamond to the traveler.
   그 행상은 인조 다이아몬드를 진짜 다이아몬드로 여행객에게 속여 팔려고 하였다.
   ** To offer for sale with intent to deceive.

8. He paid through the nose to buy his girlfriend a Rolex watch.
   롤렉스 시계를 애인에게 사주려 엄청난 돈을 지급했다.
   **To pay more for it than is fair or reasonable.

9. They may take you to the cleaners if you drink at the bar.
   그 술집에서 술을 마시면 당신을 등칠 것이다.
   ** To take most or all their money or cause them to their money through cheating them.

10. The clerk came back at the drop of a hat with the right shoes.
    직원은 맞는 신발을 즉시 가져왔다.
    ** Immediately

Pick an unfit word

A. It looks _____ to get for her wedding gift.
   ① dime a dozen ② off the rack ③ run of the mill ④ well off

B. The street vendors sell _____ designer bags at Canal street.
   ① counterfeit ② fake ③ knock-off ④ mock.

C. The actor bought a _____ watch for his fiancé at the Macy.
   ① designer ② exorbitant ③ extravagant ④ hideous

*** Answer: A-④, B-④, C-④

생활영어 쇼핑 1-2

1. The estimation is a ballpark figure until we find a defective part.
   부서진 부품(가격)을 찾을 때까지는 견적금액은 대략의 금액입니다.
   ** Tough numerical estimate.

2. We threw in a pair of socks to stop the buyer haggle.
   가격흥정을 중단시키려 양말 한 켤레를 (무료로) 집어주었다.
   ** To add some extra thing or amount with no additional charge.

3. The store carries expensive off the rack suites.
   그 가게는 비싼 기성복 양복을 가지고 있습니다.
   ** Ready-made.

4. The customer is a nit-Picker, so every clerk refused to serve her.
   직원이 그 까다로운 여자분(buyer)에게 봉사하기를 거절하였다.
   ** A nitPicker is a person who finds faults or unimportant.

5. The new phones fly off the rack.
   그 전화기는 날개 돋친 듯 팔립니다.
   ** To sell very quickly.

6. The customer drives the clerk up the wall to get a deep discount.
   그 손님은 더 값을 깎아달라고 직원을 미치게 한다.
   ** To make someone extremely angry.

7. The grass is greener on the other side.
   남의 떡이 커 보인다(남의 집 잔디가 더 파랗게 보인다).

Find an incorrect words

A. The _____ purse can go for as much as $40.
   ① a dime a dozen ② exorbitant ③ low-end ④ run of the mill

B. The street vendor hawks _____ designer bags in broad daylight.
   ① authentic ② copy-cat ③ fake ④ knock-off ⑤ pirate

*** Answer: A-②, B-①

생활영어 쇼핑 1-3

1. Touch the fabric. It speaks for itself.
   그 천을 만져 보십시오. 그 천 자체가 (질을) 말해줍니다
   ** To be so evident that no further comment is necessary.

2. The lady shelled out $250 for her hairdo at the beauty salon.
   그 숙녀는 미장원에게 250불을 억지로 지불했다. [너무 비싸서])
   ** To give money for something, usually unwillingly.

3. The girls browse around at the shopping mall.
   그여자들은 쇼핑몰에서 (사지 않고) 그냥 둘러본다.
   ** Window shopping. [not eye shopping]

4. You sold me. I will buy it.
   내가 당신의 설득력에 넘어갔으니 사겠습니다.
   **To convince or persuade one to do something or to accept some plan or idea.

5. Ring it up for me, please.
   계산해 주십시오.

6. We plan to buy our furniture on a monthly installment.
   우리는 가구를 월부로 매입할 계획이다.

7. The clerk ripped you off. They knew you were a sucker.
   당신이 봉인 줄 알고 점원이 바가지 씌웠다.

8. Exxon jacked up the gas price 40% during the Russian war in 2022.
   Exxon 정유회사는 2022년 러시아 전쟁 중 휘발유 값을 40% 올렸다.
   ** To increase the price of something suddenly.

9. $150 bucks for the leather jacket? It's a steal.
   가죽 잠바가 $150불이라고? 정말 저렴합니다.
   ** A bargain

10. Swipe the credit card or stick into the machine.
신용카드를 긁거나 카드를 밀어 넣으십시오.
카드를 읽을 수 있게 위에서 아래로 민다.

Find an unfit word

A. The outfit she wore is a(n) _____ Chanel dress.

① authentic ② bona fide ③ genuine ④ valid

*** Answer: ④

✏️ 익혀둘 만한 단어

A. Bait and switch.
세일이라고 하면서 가게에 가면 상품이 매진되었다고, 대신 비싼 상품을 보여주는 술책.

B. Lay away plan
돈이 부족해 일부 값만 주고 찾을 때 잔액을 지불하는 제도.

C. Will call
주문한 상품을 가서 찾는 것.
Will call is defined as Picking up something you've already purchased.

D. Rain check
가게에 상품이 없을 때 다음에 상품이 오면 sale 가격에 상품을 살 수 있는 쿠판(coupon).

E. Dime Store
바늘, 실 같은 작은 품목을 파는 가게.

F. Kiosk
음식을 주문하는 기계(맥도날드, 버거킹에서 햄버거 주문).

생활영어 쇼핑 1-4

1. **How do you pay for it?**
   어떻게 지불하시겠습니까(현금, 카드, 수표 etc.)?
2. **You put 30% down to order the curtain.**
   커튼을 주문하려면 30%을 선금을 내야 합니다.
3. **The mom & pop store carries comb and needles.**
   그 구멍가게에서는 빗과 바늘을 취급합니다.
4. **His mom pinches every penny to buy a car.**
   그의 어머니는 차를 산다고 일전도 아낀다.
5. **Keep the receipt in case you want to return it.**
   환불받으려면 영수증을 보관하십시오.

🔍 짝퉁 파는 시장 – 뉴욕시

Knock offs at Canal St. in NYC   서울의 이태원처럼 짝퉁 판매

짝퉁 판매하는 시장 at Canal St. @New York City

The Canal street is well-known for people trying to sell knock-off Designer items to those unknowing or knowing but not caring as long as it looks real and the price is right. "The money that is raised by the sale of these counterfeit goods, are used to further other crimes, said NYPD Deputy Chief Benjamin Gurley." "We will go wherever, and whenever, we need to go to stop these kind of crimes and furthering crime throughout our city."

Walking on Canal you'll be whispered at "Gucci, Prada or Chanel? Louis Vuitton, Coach?" If you noded the whisperer will ask you to follow him or her to a place where its not so crowded and out of sight from the police. Or you'll be asked to follow and you'll be taken to a secret store. Which is sort of scary and exciting. A back alley, or a dark stairway that leads to some basement.

N.Y. police said they seized a mountain of knock-off luxury goods with a street value of more than $10 million on Nov. 28, 2022.

2022년 경찰은 $2,000만불짜리 가짜 명품 시계, 핸드백을 압수하였다. @Lower Manhattan in N.Y. City.

미국 백화점과 백화점 숫자

A guide for shoppers in the USA.

1. 상품판매(high-end) 백화점
Bloomingdale's(85 stores), Neiman Marcus(43), Nordstrom(348), Saks 5th Avenue.

2. 중산층이 찾는 백화점
Macy (546) , Dilard's(282 stores),

3. 일반 고객이 찾는 백화점
Target(1,956), JCPenney(840), Kohl's(1,162), Sears(741), Kmart, Walmart(4,622)

4. 아웃렛 가게(Outlet stores)
Ross(1,765), T.J. Max(1,309), Marshalls(1,190)

*** 고급 백화점에서 팔다가 안 팔린 상품을 모아 다른 가게로 옮긴 곳에서 판매하는 상품: Nordstrom Rack. Bloomingdale's

Chapter 5.

패연

Fashion

생활영어 패션 1-1

1. The more the <u>melanin</u> your skin produces, the darker it gets.
   피부에 <u>색소</u>를 더 많이 만들면 피부가 더 검어진다.
   ** A dark brown to black pigment occurring in the hair, skin.

2. MSN reports that Vitamin <u>C serums</u> brighten dark spots.
   MSN 언론은 비타민C-세럼은 검은 점의 검은 색갈을 희게 만든다고 보고하였다.
   ** Clear liquid that can be separated from clotted blood.

3. Tomato: this natural cure can <u>ward off</u> bacteria that causes blisters in the first place.
   토마토: 물집이나 두드러기를 일으키는 박테리아를 <u>막아낸다</u>.
   ** To try to prevent it.

4. You can peel off or scrub dead skin with an <u>exfoliating towel</u>.
   죽은 피부를 <u>이태리 타올</u>로 벗기거나 (때처럼) 밀 수 있다.
   ** Wash cloth: Excellent for Removing Makeup and Dead Skin.

5. The sweater makes her chest <u>voluptuous</u>.
   스웨터는 그녀의 가슴을 <u>풍만하게</u> 만든다.
   ** Being full-figured and curvy.

6. <u>Liver spots</u>, also called age spots, commonly occur in people over the age of 40.
   <u>검버섯</u>은 40살이 넘으면 대체로 나타난다.
   ** Small, flat dark areas on the skin.

7. Some bacterial <u>acne</u> grows with dead skin and oil in pores.
   <u>여드름</u>은 숨구멍에 죽은 피부와 기름으로 균이 자란 것.

생활영어 패션 1-2

1. Dressing up for orchestra concerts went out of the window in the late 80s.
   오케스트라 연주 때 정장 입는 것은 1980년경에 사라졌다.
   ** Disappear.

2. She thinks she is a swan among ducks.
   그녀는 자기가 군계일학이라고 생각한다.

3. 90% of male suites are off the rack.
   남자 양복의 90%는 기성복이다.
   ** Ready-made rather than made to order.

4. Couturier Lifshitz is the owner of Polo.
   남자 디자이너 L은 폴로 회사 주인이다.

5. Buy a fire retardant night gown for your baby.
   아기의 잠옷은 불이 잘 붙지 않는 잠옷을 구매하십시오.
   ** A substance that is used to slow down or stop the spread of fire or reduce its intensity.

6. It is hard to tell which one is a knock-off designer bag.
   어느 것이 가짜 명품 가방인지 모르겠다.

생활영어 패션 1-3

1. Clipping double eyelid surgery costs 1,800 dollars in Korea.
   한국에서 쌍꺼풀 수술하는 데 $1,800 든다.

2. Asian females get cosmetic surgery to get a pointed nose.
   코를 뾰족하게 올리려고 동양 여성들은 성형수술을 한다.

3. He parts his hair left.
   그는 가르마를 왼쪽으로 탄다.

4. Her gaudy outfits turn her friend off.
   그녀의 야한 옷이 친구들 입맛 떨어지게 한다.
   ** showy, bright and definitely tacky.

5. Tease my hair a bit higher.
   ** a styling technique that can be used to add volume and texture to your hair.

6. Wear a solid blouse because your skirt with big flower pattern is too loud.
   스카트의 꽃무늬가 너무 요란해서 단색 블라우스를 입으세요.
   ** Solid color(단색). Loud: 요란한.

7. Flat front pants are in, pleated pants are out.
   주름있는 바지는 들어가고 주름없는 바지가 유행이다.
   ** a fold in cloth made by doubling material over on itself.

8. She thinks she is a swan among ducks.
   그녀는 자기가 군계일학이라고 생각한다.

9. The aging actress decided to get a facelift for her sagging skin.
   나이 든 여배우는 축 처진 얼굴의 피부를 당기는 수술을 하려 결정을 했다.
   **Drooping down from weight.

10. She wears a petite size.
    그 여성은 체구가 작은 여성을 위해 만든 작은 옷을 입는다.
    ** Short and having a small, trim figure.

11. His mom buys husky size pants for her overweight kid.
    그 어머니는 비대한 아이를 위해 비대한 크기의 바지를 산다.
    **Made in a size meant for the larger or heavier than average boy.

12. Alaskans wear thermal underwear in October.
    알래스카 사람들은 10월에 속내의를 입는다.

13. She wears a long dress to camouflage her bow legs.
    그 여성은 휜 다리를 감추려 긴 드레스를 입는다.
    ** concealment by means of digukse.

14. The sweater makes her chest voluptuous.
    스웨터는 그녀의 가슴을 풍만하게 만든다

15. She shows off her sexy legs with a slit skirt.
    그 여성은 터진 스카트로 섹시한 다리를 자랑한다.
    ** to have in a way that is intended to attract attention or admiration.

16. The boy looks preppy with a tweed blazer.
    상의를 입은 학생은 귀티나게 보인다.
    ** Prep. school에서 나온 단어.

Find an unfit word

A. She always keeps her hair _____.

① curly ② kinky ③ savvy ④ wavy

B. The girls are too busy to _____ their legs and facial hair for the party.

① divert ② pluck ③ shave ④ wax

C. Her dress pattern is _____.

① checkered ② opal ③ plaid ④ polka dot

D. He was at the party, dressed in a(n) _____ shirts with khaki pants.

① oxford ② polo ③ Tee ④ Y

E. You should _____ it on, and see whether it fits.

① get ② put ③ slip ④ throw

F. She used to put on _____ during the summer vacation.

① big smile ② hair ③ heavy makeup ④ some weight

G. If you _____ a thick make-up, you can create a pore clogging situation.

① apply ② put on ③ take ④ wear

*** Answer: A-③, B-①, C-②, D-④, E-①, F-②, G-③

Fashion or Show-Off

A) Long neck is fashion

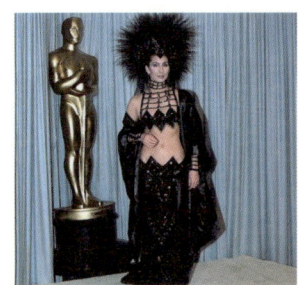

B) Cher at Oscar

In some part of Africa

　소비자들의 패션에(fashon) 대한 성향을 보려고 L 대학이 아마존 상품 10,000점을 명품과 유명세 없는 상품을 섞어 놓은 것에 대한 소비자의 반응을 보았다. 패션에 대한 미(美)적인 패션보다는 권위적인(prestgious) 명품을 (Luxury Brand) 그저 멋진(fashionable) 것으로 보아 넘긴다고 그 대학이 발표하였다.

　What our studies showed is that perceptions of Fashion forwardness of being in the know-can outweigh aesthetics when choosing a luxury brand item. Ugly has somehow become a signal of taste, of the good life of luxury and prestige. "Consumers trust a product from all luxury brand, assuming it has positive qualities, rather than questioning it," Cesareo says. "If something is from a luxury brand, then it is fashionable." Thus, luxury brands don't need to follow prescribed norms. Consumers who perceive an item as luxurious also assume that it costs more.

　To test their theory, Cesareo and colleagues conducted a series of studies with university students, online Mechanical Turk workers and Amazon customers to consider a range of product categories and multiple luxury and non-luxury brands. They manipulated the aesthetics of real luxury and non-Luxury products, as well as a single product styled in different ways, and included more than 10,000 Amazon products. Amazon data.

〈Lehigh University〉

Chapter 6.
데이트 & 결혼

Date & Marriage

생활영어 데이트

1. The boy met a girl and fell head-over-heels at a prom.
   그 아이는 고등학교 파티에서 여학생을 만나자 사랑에 빠졌다.
   ** Fall in love.

2. She is shacking up with her boss who has a wife.
   그녀는 유부남 상사와 동거생활을 하고 있다.
   ** To move in to shared accommodation with someone, generally of the opposite sex for purposes of sexual intercourse.

3. Later, he knocked her up during the summer vacation.
   그 후, 그는 그녀를 여름방학 때 임신시켰다.
   ** Make a woman pregnant.

4. The girl's mom blamed the guy for her pregnancy, in fact, It takes two to tango.
   여자 어머니는 그 사내를 탓하지만, 실은 두 손이 마주쳐야 소리가 난다.
   ** Some activities require two participating parties and can not be done alone.

5. He made a pass at his co-worker.
   그는 직장 여성 동료에게 (관계 맺으려) 찝쩍였다.
   ** do something that clearly shows one wants to begin a romantic or sexual relationship with (someone).

6. He just asked your name. Cat got your tongue?
   그가 단지 당신의 이름을 물어보는데 왜 입을 다물지?
   ** an expression that is used when someone is quiet and isn't talking or responding when you expect them to.

7. Darn it ! Ms. Kim stood me up again.
   젠장! 미스 김이 나를 또 바람 맞췄다.

8. The town is well known that guys can Pick up chicks for <u>one night stand</u>.

   그 동네는 <u>하룻밤</u> 잘 여자를 찾기 쉬운 동네로 알려졌다.

   ** a sexual relationship lasting only one night.

9. The guy must have been wearing <u>beer goggles</u> when he asked a broad for a date at the bar.

   그 사내가 술집에서 그 여성에게 데이트 신청한 것보면 술을 많이 마셔 <u>눈에 콩깍지가 낀</u> 것이 분명하다.

   ** A person has been drinking so much alcohol that they think someone is more sexually attractive.

10. After She found out that her boyfriend was <u>two-timing</u> her with the woman next door, she dumped him.

    그 여성은 남자 애인이 <u>다른 여성(옆집)과 date</u> 하는 걸 알고 그를 버렸다.

    ** **To betray** (a spouse or lover) by secret date with another. [두 사람과 date하다]

Pick an incorrect word

A. The famous Dolly Parton's _____ was the talk of the town.

   ① boobs ② bosom ③ butts ④ tits

B. His high school girlfriend is _____.

   ① babe ② fox ③ hottie ④ knockout ⑤ slut

C. He has been _____ to female coworkers.

   ① advancing ② coming on ③ deriding ④ hitting on

D. The girls went nuts when the _____ showed up at the party.

   ① dude ② hood ③ hunk ④ stud

** Answer: A-③, B-⑤, C-③, D-②

Connect the related words

A. Dream   ① bait

B. Gold   ② boat

C. Jail   ③ chaser

D. Skirt   ④ daddy

E. Sugar   ⑤ digger

** Answer: A-②, B-⑤, C-①, D-③, E-④

🔍 중매와 데이트

A) 중매 – 상해, 중국

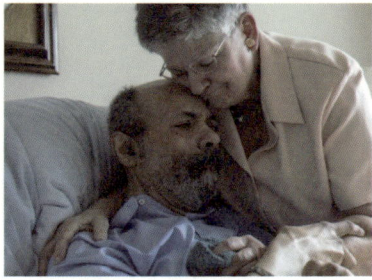
B) Long Waiting for love

A) 중국 상해나 북경에서는 자식들을 결혼시키려고 주말이 되면 부모들이 공원에 모여 자식들의 학력, 키, 직장, 사진을 넣은 이력서를(?) 파라솔 위에 얹어 놓는다.
결혼시킬 자식들의 2/3는 대졸, 나이는 20~30세가 제일 많다고 함.

B) 대학생 시절 시카고에서 데이트 하던 중 남자 애인이 흑인이라고 여성 집에서 반대하여 헤어지고 40여 년이 지난 후, 여성이 시카고에 찾아와 아픈 흑인 애인을 찾아와 다시 결혼하였다.

Parents seemingly attend the park because they see it as a way of fulfilling their parental duties, and also possibly because it is an opportunity to voice and discuss their dissatisfactions – about their unmarried children, what they see as the excessive demands of other parents, and what many perceive this as a 'crisis' of marriage in China.

Matchmaking and marriage in modern China | Pursuit
by the University of Melbourne (unimelb.edu.au)

🔍 PBS-TV

In a country of 1.3 billion people, it's not always easy to meet Mr. or Miss Right.

That's why on Saturday and Sunday afternoons, parents congregate in a corner of People's Park, a sanctuary of palm trees, ponds and winding paths in the heart of this busy Chinese city. Lining the brick pathways are hundreds of pastel umbrellas on which these well-meaning parents have clipped information about their sons' and daughters' age, height, weight, occupation and level of education.

China's 'marriage market' where mom sets you up on your first date | PBS News

🔍 Cuffing Season

한국에는 "봄바람 난다" 와 색다른 영어단어로, 봄이 아니고 가을, 겨울 때 바람나는 단어인데, 춥고 외로워선지(?) 11월부터 3월초에 나타난다고 함.

"cuffing season" is the time of year when the weather starts to turn cooler and people start seeking relation-ships to get them.

🔍 로맨스 사기: FTC 미국정부 보고서

로맨스를 빙자하여 미국에서 70,000만 건 사기가 발생했고, 2022년 이 사기로 $17억 피해를 보았다.

Romance scammers' favorite lies. 2월 9일, 2023.

Romance scammers tell all sorts of lies to steal your heart and money, and reports to the FTC show those lies are working. Last year's romance scam numbers looked a lot like 2021 all over again, and it's not a pretty picture. In 2022, nearly 70,000 people reported a romance scam, and reported losses hit a staggering $1.3 billion. you want to meet in real life, and they can't. Reports show their excuse is often baked right into their fake identity.

Claiming to be a faraway military base is the most popular excuse, but "offshore oil rig worker" is another common (and fake) occupation.

Chapter 7.

식당

Restaurant

생활영어　식당

1. Wait until the waitress seats all 4 of us.
   웨이트레스가 4명을 좌석에 앉혀 줄 때까지 기다리십시오.

2. The chef makes the sausage from scratch here.
   그 요리사는 소시지를 처음부터 이곳에서 만든다.
   ** From the very beginning.

3. The ribeye steak melts in my mouth.
   등심 스테이크는 입에서 살살 녹는다(맛있다).
   ** Delicious.

4. The meat of the pork cutlet tastes like cardboard.
   돈가스 고기는 마분지 같다(오래된 고기).
   ** 부드럽지 않고 오래된 소고기, 생선들은 주스가(juice, 육즙) 말라버린 상태.

5. He is still working on it. Don't take his dish away.
   아직도 먹는 중이니 그의 접시를 치우지 마십시오.
   ** 먹는 중을 work on 단어로 사용함.

6. Put extra ketchup, but hold the mustard on my hot dog.
   내 핫도그에는 케첩을 더 넣지만 겨자는 넣지 마십시오.
   ** hold가 넣지 말라는 의미.

7. Costco sells a rotisserie chicken for $5.99.
   코스트코는 통닭구이를 $5.99에 판다.
   ** A special kind of oven that keeps meat turning constantly as it cooks.

8. Koreans eat red-bean puree on the winter solstice.
   한국인은 동짓날에 팥죽을 먹는다.
   ** a very smooth, crushed or blended food.

9. The kid has a sweet tooth. Don't take him to a candy store.

    그 아이는 단것을 좋아한다. 사탕 파는 가게에 데려가지 말아라.

    ** A great liking for sweet-tasting foods.

10. Flax seeds have omega-3 that reduces heart attack.

    삼베 씨앗에는 심장병을 감소시키는 오메가-3 성분이 있다.

11. Tapas is Spanish food. Most customers order 3~5 dishes Because it has a small amount of food.

    타파스는 스페인 요리이며, 양이 적어 3~5 요리를 주문한다.

12. The chef sautes onion to make onion rings.

    그 요리사는 양파링을 만들려고 잠시 기름에 튀긴다.

    ** To fry food in a small amount of oil or butter.

13. Gyros is a Greek sandwich meat which is mix of lamb, pork, and veal.

    기로스는 샌드위치에 넣는 양, 돼지, 소고기를 섞은 그리스 고기이다.

    ** Gyros is one of the most popular Greek street food dishes, consisting of meat such as pork and chicken (in Greece) or lamb and veal. 이제 미국에서 자주 볼 수 있다.

14. Spicy Cajun food came from Louisiana State with influence of French Immigrant.

    매운 케이준 음식은 불란서 이민자의 영향을 받은 루이지아나주 음식.

    ** Jambalaya, Gumbos는 이제 L.A, Las Vegas, Chicago, NYC에서도 볼 수 있고, 식당 chain BJ's에서 사 먹을 수 있다.

Pick an unfit word

A. The girl is a bit more _____ than her brother.
① finicky ② fussy ③ lanky ④ Picky

B. The smell of BBQ ribs makes us _____ when we pass there.
① drool ② salivate ③ swoon ④ water.

C. Mike had a _____ meal, a shank, a size of George Foreman's fist.
① hearty ② scanty ③ square ④ sumptuous

D. She knows how to make perfect _____ eggs.
① flat ② over easy ③ scrambled ④ sunny side-up

*** Answer: A-③, B-③, C-②, D-①

Connect words that are related

A. calamari   ① 치즈

B. cheddar   ② 조개

C. scallops   ③ 버섯

D. truffle   ④ 오징어

E. zucchini   ⑤ 호박

*** Answer: A-④, B-①, C-②, D-③, E-⑤

Connect words that are related

A. Calamari   ① giardiniera

B. Hot dog   ② maple syrup

C. Italian beef   ③ marinara

D. Nacho   ④ relish

E. Pan cake   ⑤ salsa

*** Answer: A- ③, B- ④, C- ①, D- ⑤, E- ②

🔍 자주 듣는 식당 문장

1. Soybean paste is fermented soybean.
   된장은 콩을 발효시킨 음식이다.
2. Most of Neng-Myun is buck-wheat noodles in icy beef broth.
   대부분 냉면은 찬 소고기 육수에 메밀 국수를 넣은 음식이다.
3. Bool-go-kee is sliced beef marinated(with soy sauce, garlic and fruit juice such as apple or pear.)
   불고기는 얇게 썬 소고기를 양념에 절인 것이다.
4. The entrée comes with 4 side dishes.
   정식에는 4가지 반찬이 같이 나온다.
   ** bread and soup(or salade), baked(or mashed) potato, and green beans.
5. Kebab is grilled meat and vegetables on a skewer.
   꼬치(산적)는 꼬챙이에 채소와 고기를 구운 것이다.
   ** 일본, 미국, 한국은 고기를 꼬챙이에 끼워 굽지만, 유럽, 그리스 같은 곳에서는 고기 대신 Gyros 고기를 사용한다.

   기로스(Gyros): 돼지고기, 닭고기, 소고기, 양고기 등을 섞어서 갈아 큰 덩어리로 만든 것. 저질의 고기를 섞어 만들어 유럽에서 판매 금지를 당할 뻔하였다.

🔍 Scoville Scale(매운 고추 강도 측정)

1. Bell pepper · · · · · · · · · 0도
2. Banana pepper · · · · · · · · 0 ~ 500도
3. Anaheim · · · · · · · · · · 1,000 ~ 2,500도
4. Jalapeno · · · · · · · · · · 2,500~ 8,000도
5. Tabasco · · · · · · · · · · 25,000~50,000도
6. Cayenne · · · · · · · · · · 30,000~50,000도
7. Habanero · · · · · · · · · 100,000~350,000도
8. Ghost pepper · · · · · · · 1,000,000도
9. Carolina Reaper · · · · · · 2,200,000도
10. Apollo Pepper · · · · · · · 3,000,000도

** 파프리카(Paprika): 이 단어는 고춧가루라는 단어이며, 고추는 피망(Bell Pepper)이다.

🔍 1970년 이후 식당 동향

1970여 년 후반부터 미국이 동양인 이민을 받기 시작하자, 중국의 기름기 많은 Mandarin, Cantonese 식당들이 줄어들고 매운 음식을 만드는 중국 남부지역 세지완(Sichuan, 四川省) 음식, 멕시코, 태국 음식점이 많이 증가하고, 초밥, 생선회 파는 일본 식당들이 증가하였다.

이제 미국에는 기름기 많은 중국음식인 Mandarin, Cantonese 식당들은 많이 줄고, 멕시코 식당이 많아졌다. 베트남과 태국 식당들이 가격도 저렴하여 많이 증가하였다. 이제는 중국식당(Panda Express) 체인은 2,200여 개가 넘고, 커피집 스타벅스가 36,000여 개로 전 세계로 퍼지자, 한국의 파리 바게트와 Tous les Jours, 대만의 85°C Bakery 가게가 우리 한인 동네에도 나타났다. 아직도 햄버거, 샌드위치, 닭요리 식당이 대다수지만 이태리 피자, 스파게티, 라자니아(Lasagne), 멕시코의 타코, 버리도(Burrito)가 외국 음식으로 인기가 높아졌다.

A) Lofoten(노르웨이) codfish   B) 중국 Hunan성

A) Stockfish is unsalted fish, especially cod, dried by the cold and wind in Norway. wooden racks (which are called "hjell" in Norway) on the foreshore.
B) 중국(Sichuan, Hunan)에서는 매운 고추 먹기 시합에서 버티겠다고 물속에서 경기까지 하고 있다. 유럽, 미국은 30분 내 매운 고추(habanero)를 많이 먹는 자가 챔피언이 된다. 매운 고추 먹기 대회에서는 주로 habanero 고추를 대회에 쓰며, 미국 식품점(Albertsons)에서 몇 년 전부터 판매 시작, 매운 소스로 한국에서 초고추장처럼 중국의 시라챠(Sriracha), 이태리의 쟈리에나(Giardiniera), 멕시코의 살사(Salsa)가 토비스코(Tabasco)가 인지도를 넘어 대중어(household name)가 되어간다.

🔍 생선 서브하는 식당

미국 중부는 생선을 잘 먹지 않고 중국음식점도 Nyc, Lax지역보다 적다. 70년 경에는 뉴욕과 시카고의 Fulton Market 같이 큰 생선시장들이 있어 소라(Conch Chowder)도 잘 먹었는데…, 게(Dungeness) 사먹기도 힘들다. 민물고기로는 Perch, 메기(Catfish)는 식품점에서 보인다.

영국에서 많이 보이는 Fish & Chip 음식이 미국에서는 Long John Silver's나 찾아가야 생선을 먹을수 있는데, 이제는 태국식당(Boiling Crab)에서 대게, 새우가 있고, 미국 전역에 있는 유명한 이태리 식당 Magiano에는 오징어(Calamari), 또 해물 스파게티(Frutti Di Mare) 요리에 조개, 오징어, 새우, 가리비(Scallop)가 있다. 오래된 식당(Red Lobster)에도 새우, 랍스터가 있다. 일본 생선회 유행 전 미국 술집에서 생굴을 팔았다.

색다른 남부 New Orleans의 요리인 케젼(Cajun) 음식 잠바라야 (Jambalaya) 요리를 Bj's 식당(Chain)에서 판다.

게(Dungeness)가 많이 잡히는 서부 해변 오레곤주, 워싱턴주(Sfo-Eugene-Portland-Seattle) 해변을 따라 800여 마일을 여행해도 맛있는 게(Dungeness)를 요리해주는 식당 찾기가 무척 힘들었다.

아직까지 미국에서 이태리 식당이 생선요리를 제일 많이 한다.

오징어 튀김(calamari), 새우요리(Scampy), 해물 스파게티(Spaghetti allo Scoglio), 생선찌개(Cioppino(stew)). 이태리를 여행하면 피자(topping)에 멸치(anchovy)를 종종 본다.

매운 음식과 한국의 초고추장 같은 소스

매운 초고추장 같은 소스를 뿌려 먹는 식당으로는 중국 식당(Panda Express, 2,300개 chain)이 미국 전국에 퍼져 있고, 초고추장 같은 중국산 고추장(Sriracha)과 멕시코식당 Taco Bell 같은 곳에 나초(nacho)나 타코에 넣는 살사(Salsa)가 인기 높다. 뉴올리언스의 매운 소스는 많은 식당에 비치됨.

한국 고추장과 비슷한 중국 남부의 유난, 하남지역과 고추장 공장(Chengdu)은 어마어마한 규모로 생산하고 있다.

미국은 돼지갈비(back-rib)의 BBQ, 체인점(chain) 식당인 Lucille's이나 Famous Dave's 식당 식탁에는 맵거나 단맛의 BBQ 소스가 네 다섯 개가 비치되어 있다. 간장 공장은 일본의 기코만이 위스킨신(Wisconsin) 주에서 생산하며 전 세계로 판매하고 있다.

미쉐린 식당 리뷰(Michelin Restaurant review)

(불란서 회사가 세계의 식당을 리뷰) April / 2022

불란서 타이어 회사가 1921년 세계 식당의 맛과 서비스를 별 한 개부터 3개로 평점을 주기 시작하여 세계의 대도시 식당들이 별 두 개만 받으면 큰 덕을 보고 있다. 일본 동경은 미쉐린 별 한 개 받은 식당이 150개로 5개 대도시에 올라섰다.

While the Michelin brand is globally well-known for its tires, the Paris-based company is also famous for its annual Michelin Guide Michelin stars are now considered a hall- mark of fine dining by many of the world's top chefs - not to mention restaurant patrons. Not easy to obtain, the stars are awarded to restaurants that Michelin considers the very best in a given city.

How Does a Restaurant Get a Michelin Star?

First, the Michelin Guide team will select a number of restaurants in specific locations to be inspected by an anonymous reviewer. After the inspector visits the selected restaurant, they write a comprehensive report about the total culinary experience, including the quality and presentation of the dishes, among other rating criteria outlined below.

The group of Michelin inspectors will the meet to analyze the reports and discuss in-depth which restaurants are worthy of a Michelin Star (or two or three). In 1931, the rating system expanded to become the Michelin three-star rating that continues today. Unlike most star rating systems, one star is not a bad thing.

미쉐린 상 받은 제일 저렴한 음식 포장마차집

The world's cheapest Michelin-starred meal in Singapore.One such hawker stall is Hill Street Tai Hwa Pork Noodle,a street-food vendor that sells a Michelin-starred dish for Singapore dollars($4.50).

도시별 미쉐린 상 받은 음식점

City	3 stars	2 stars	1 star
Paris	10	17	10(2023)
Tokyo	12	42	150(2021)
London	5	12	57(2023)
N.Y. City	5	13	46(2021)

국가별 2022년

France: 758, Japan: 554, Italy: 432, Germany: 384, United States: ?

** 불란서의 Michelin tire 회사가 1936년부터 식당 Review.

Chapter 8.
나이트 클럽

Bar or Nightclub

생활영어 술집 1-1

1. At the party, she drank with the guy under the table.
   파티에서 그 여성은 그 남자보다 술이 셌다.
   ** To drink more alcohol than (someone else) without becoming extremely drunk, unconscious, etc.

2. He went cold turkey after the DUI arrest.
   음주로 체포당한 후 단호하게 술을 끊었다.
   ** To stop doing something completely.

3. Drink it in one go.
   그것을 한 번에 다 마셔라.   ** one attempt. 비슷한 단어: bottoms up.

4. After finishing half a bottle of whisky, he went off the rails.
   위스키 반병을 끝낸 후 그는 제정신이 아니었다.
   ** To start behaving in a way that is not generally acceptable.

5. He said he quits drinking. It is hog wash.
   그가 술을 끊는다는 말은 헛소리이다.
   ** Ridiculous speech. Nonsense.

6. He spilled the beans about his ex-wife's family after he got drunk.
   술에 취하자 그는 전 부인 가족에 대한 비밀을 터트렸다.
   **reveal secret information.

7. Her husband has been in the dog house since he blew his entire pay-check at the strip club.
   남편이 성인 클럽에서 한 달 월급을 다 날리고 곤경에 처했다.
   ** In a situation in which someone is angry at you.

8. He had beer goggles yesterday, hitting on the chick.
   시원찮은 여성이 멋지게 보여 찝쩍이는 것 보면 어제 그는 술에 취했다. [평범한 여성이 술때문에 멋지게 보임]
   ** consumption of alcohol makes physically unattractive persons appear beautiful.
   ** hit on : flirt with someone.

9. He fell off the wagon after his wife passed away.
   그는 부인이 사망하고 술중독에 다시 빠졌다.
   ** To return to drinking alcohol after a period of abstinence

10. The "AABB", one of the notorious club house chain, charged $125,000 to a drunk customer. They took him to the cleaners.
    클럽하우스 chain인 "AABB"는 술취한 손님에게 $ 12.5만 불 바가지를 씌웠다(털렸다).
    ** To cheat or swindle one for a lot or all of their money.

Pick an unfit word

A. The girls meet at the joint to _____ every Friday.
   ① blow the whistle ② chew the fat ③ chit chat ④ shoot the breeze

B. He got _____ last week. Don't rub him up the wrong way.
   ① Cut it out ② Knock it off ③ Lay off ④ shrug off

*** Answer: A-①, B-④

Pick an unfit word

A. His son can not drink any _____ until he turns 21.
   ① booze ② bubbly ③ Irish coffee ④ root beer

B. He goes to the _____ bar every Friday to meet his buddy.
   ① cocktail ② keg ③ oyster ④ piano ⑤ sports

C. BJ's restaurants carry _____ beers.
   ① ale ② draft ③ rauger ④ root

D. His girlfriend drinks like a _____ .
   ① boozer ② fish ③ hunk ④ sailor

*** Answer: A-④, B-②, C-④, D-③

생활영어 술집 1-2

1. The boozers start with boiler makers.
   술고래들은 폭탄주로 시작한다.
   ** A shot of whiskey followed by a glass of beer as a chaser.

2. The bar is a clip joint.
   그 술집은 바가지 씌우는 집이다.
   ** Night club, or bar where customers are regularly overcharged.

3. One pitcher of beer is 12 bucks at the honky tonk.
   그 선술집은 한 피처 맥주가 12불이다.
   ** Cheap bar, club, or dance hall. 1 pitcher = 48 oz.

4. Put it on my tab for her drink.
   그녀의 술은 내 계산서에 달아라.
   ** Bill.

5. He can drink a 6 pack of beer in one sitting.
   그 사람은 한 번 앉은 자리에서 6병 술을 끝낼 수 있다.

6. Order your drink now; it is the last call.
   술을 시키십시오. (문 닫기 전) 마지막 술 주문입니다.

7. The stingy boss Picked up the tab.
   짠돌이 상사가 계산하였다.

8. His wife took it out on us for his alcoholism.
   그 부인은 남편이 술중독 된 것을 우리에게 화풀이했다.
   ** The expression to "take something out" on someone used when we treat someone badly because of our motions (usually anger).

9. Get me a beer on tap, please.
   술통(kag)에 있는 맥주를 주세요.
   ** beer being poured directly into a glass from a large container. 값이 저렴함.

10. She gets screw loose whenever she hits the bottle.
    그 여성은 술만 마시면 나사가 빠진다.
    ** Behave in a strange way or crazy.

11. They wet their whistle at the bar after work.
    그들은 퇴근 후 그 술집에서 술을 마신다.
    ** Have a drink.

12. Next round is on me.
    다음 순배(순서)는 내가 낸다.

13. This drink is on the house.
    이번 술은 술집주인이 한턱내는 술이다.
    ** Something is paid for as a courtesy of the owner.

14. He takes a Bloody Mary for his hang-over.
    그는 숙취 때 칵테일 bloody Merry를 마신다.
    ** The experience of unpleasant physiological and Psychological effects usually following the consumption of alcohol.

15. He flips out whenever he takes more than 3 drinks.
    그가 3잔 이상 마시기만 하면 헤까닥한다(뒤집어진다).
    ** To become crazy, very excited, or angry.

16. Put her drink on my tab
    그녀의 술은 내 계산서에 올리십시오.
    ** To add a charge to one's bill when buying a product usually a food or drink.

17. Let's go Dutch! Separate check here please!
    각자 냅시다. 각자 계산서를 여기에 주시오.
    ** 한국에서 말하는 dutch pay/ pay separately.

18. The joint has been our hang-out since college.
    그 장소는 대학시절부터 우리들의 단골집이었다.
    ** A favorite place to spend time.

19. He spiked the fruit cocktail with 80 proof vodka at the party.
   그는 파티에서 과일 칵테일에 80도 보드카로 강하게 높였다.
   ** Add alcohol or a drug to contaminate(drink or food)

20. It's getting late. Cheers, One for The Road, bottoms up!
   늦어집니다. 건배. 떠나기 전 마지막 한잔합시다. 한 번에 다 마시자.

> 🔍 Studio 54 @ NYC in the 1970s.(1977~1980)

Cher & Rod Stuart. @ 54

Studio 54 @ NYC in the 1970s

    1,006석을 가진 이 나이트-클럽은 1977년경 가장 유명한 디스코 술집으로 알려졌다. 뉴욕시에서 제일 유명한 세레버리티 Richard Gere, Elizabeth Taylor, Al Pacino, Mick Jagger, Liza Minnelli, Cher들의 "the celebrity playground."
마약과 섹스 스캔들로 문을 닫았다.
    Studio 54 was the hottest party spot in the world, defining the disco era in all its ecstasy and excess. It drew the likes of Cher, Liza Minelli, Michael Jackson,, Liz Taylor....and so many More from the global A-List of Celebrity in the late '70's.

    CBS

    Studio 54 is the one nightclub from the '70's everyone remembers. For most of his life, though, co-founder Ian Schrager has wanted to forget it. "I don't have only good memories. I have bittersweet memories. It was an

embarrassment to me. It still is," Schrager told "CBS This Morning: Saturday" co-host Anthony Mason.
What happened at Studio 54 is still an "embarrassment" for
For 33 months, Studio 54 was the giddy epicenter of '70's Hedonism, a disco hothouse of beautiful people, endless cocaine, and every kind of sex. Its co-owners Steve Rubell and Ian Schrager kicked off the age of the one-name celebrity
—Cher, Andy, Bianca, Halston—and rode a miraculous wave of power and pleasure until it brought them crashing down

Studio 54's Cast List: A Who's Who the 1970s Night life Circuit | Vanity Fair

🔍 기초 포도주 – 101

백 포도주	적 포도주
Full bodied white wine: Chardonnay Light bodied white wine: Pinot Gris Sweet white wine: Chenin Blanc Dry white wine: Sauvignon Blanc	Full bodied red wine: Cabernet Sauvignon Medium bodied Red wine: Grenache Light bodied red wine: Pinot Noir Sweet red wine: Dolce Dry red wine: Sauvignon Sparkling wine is Champagne

*** House wine: 식당에서 선택해서 파는 포도주
*** Full bodied: 걸직한, Thick and rich.
*** Light bodied: 맑은, Smooth and easy to drink.
*** Dry: 닳지 않은(not sweet)

 Wine 가격은 $10 ~ 50이며 Walmart, Costco 가면 한 병에 $15 가격이면 수십 가지 포도주가 있다. 그런데 왜 그렇게 비쌀까? 겨울 Xmas 때면 Univ. Of Chicago에서 일하는 직원들이 두세 번 파티할 때 와인에 관해 물으면 한 의대 교수의 말로는 자기는 한 병에 선물로도 35불 이상의 포도주를 산 적이 없다고 말했다.

🔍 칵테일

우리가 오래 살던 중서부에서 제일 많이 마시는 칵테일로 여성은 마가리타, 남자는 마티니인데, 타 주로 방문할 때 보면 2,000년경부터 새로운 이름들이 많이 나타났다. 신기한 일은 한국은 비싼 스카치위스키가 높은 지위를 차지하는데 미국인들은 바트카로 칵테일을 만들어 마셔서 그런지 바트카와 포도주를 많이 마시는 편이다. 독일에서 Wine을 마시면 가격이 높고, 블란서에서 맥주를 마시면 가격이 비싼데, 한국은 어떤지 궁금하다.

많이 마시는 칵테일 이름

1. Margarita
2. Martini
3. Old fashioned
4. Manhattan
5. Aperol Spritz
6. Moscow Mule
7. Mimosa
8. White Russian
9. Mai Tai
10. Whiskey Sour

2024년 평균 칵테일 가격은 12불이라고 Forbes가 보도하였다. 우리가 사는 변두리 가격은 $6~8. Vegas 중심가 호텔에 자주 들르는 후배는 기업인과 만날 때 칵테일이 $25불, 맥주가 15불이라고….

🔍 영국인의 한 모습 – Social Issues Research Center

Another baffled visitor asked "What is it with you British? Why do you have to play all these silly games? Why can't you just go to a bar and have a drink and talk like the rest of the world?"

The answer is that the rest of the world is not as socially inhibited and inept as the British. We don't find it easy to initiate friendly conversation with strangers, or to develop closer relationships with fellow pub goers. We need help. We need props. We need excuses to make contact. We need toys and games that get us involved with each other.

We need to throw balls and darts together and push little objects around on tables together and keep scores and exclaim over wins and grumble about losses and argue about the rules. OK?

🔍 국가별 술 소비량

Russia: 20.9
USA: 13.9
France: 7.0
Japan : 3.4

South Korea: 13.9
Czech : 13.3
Denmark: 7.5

WHO정보, 2016년

🔍 남성 술 중독자

Below are the top countries in the world with the high rate of alcohol use disorder in males: 2021.

- Russia   (16.29%)
- Hungary   (15.29%)
- Lithuania   (13.35%)
- South Korea   (13.10%)
- Latvia   (11.54%)
- Belarus   (11.43%)
- Estonia   (11.09%)
- Niue   (10.58%)
- Colombia   (10.33%)

2021(abbeycarefoundation.com)

Chapter 9.

파티

Party

생활영어 파티 1-1

1. It is an open bar before the diner party starts.
   저녁식사 전(파티 때)까지는 술이 무료이다.
   ** 일정한 시간만 bar에서 무료로 술을 제공.

2. I have his name right on the tip of my tongue.
   그의 이름이 입에서 맴돈다.
   ** Almost remembered.

3. A few waiters walk around with hors d'oeuvre until a dinner the party starts to serve customers.
   저녁 식사가 시작되기 전까지 몇 명의 웨이터들이 손님들에게 오더브(술안주? Or appetizer)를 서브하러 들고 돌아다닌다.
   ** A small dish served before before dinner.
   [Tapas, egg roll, porogi, cheese 등을 서브함.]

4. She is too shy to break the ice at the party.
   그는 수줍어서 파티에 분위기를 만들기에는 힘들다.
   **Do or say something to relieve tension.
   처음 대화를 트지 못하는…

5. Stay clear of him, He is a backstabber.
   그를 멀리하시오. 그자는 등 뒤에서 욕하는 놈이다
   ** To avoid some-one or something.

6. The party is in full swing.
   파티는 지금 한창이다.
   ** At the height of activity.

7. They pitched in for a farewell party.
   그들은 송별회를 위해 서로 돈을 내었다.

8. Hi! Make yourself at home.
   안녕, 편안히 계십시오. [긴장하지 말고 relax]

** To relax and make yourself comfortable.

9. The couple gave him the cold shoulder.
   그 부부는 그에게 차겁게(냉대) 대했다.
   ** Deliberate coldness or disregard, a slight or snub

10. His name doesn't ring a bell.
    그 사람 이름은 생소하다.
    ** To sound familiar. [부정사로 사용하면]

11. The guy called us names when we ignored his question.
    우리가 그의 질문을 무시하자 우리에게 불쾌한 말을 하였다.
    ** To mock or insult one with rude or offensive names.
    [거짓말쟁이, 사기꾼 같은 단어]

12. After a few shots of whisky, they let it all hang out.
    몇 잔의 위스키를 마신후 그들은 긴장을 풀었다.
    ** Be very relaxed. [싱거운 말도 한다.]

13. The baby shower was given for her friend.
    아기 출산 파티는 친구들이 해주었다.
    ** 지인들이 유아 출산 전 아기가 필요한 용품을 선물로 주려는 모임 겸 파티.

Pick an unfit word

A. He always _____ his hand first to shake hands with his guest.
   ① extends ② pitches ③ puts out ④ reachs

B. The guy _____ his arm around his friend's shoulder.
   ① flung ② grab ③ put ④ throw ⑤ wrap

C. Long time no see _____ in touch, buddy!
   ① connect ② keep ③ get ④ stay

*** Answer: A-②, B-②, C-①

Connect matching name

A. Bill
B. Bob
C. Dick
D. Lize
E. Ted

1. Edward.
2. Elizabeth
3. Richard
4. Robert
5. William

***Answer: A-⑤, B-④, C-③, D-②, E-①

Connect related words

A. Dumb
B. Lazy
C. Sleepy
D. Slow
E. Smarty

1. Poke
2. Pants
3. Head
4. Bone
5. Bell

***Answer: A-⑤, B-④, C-③, D-①, E-②

생활영어 파티 1-2

1. His friend gave him a <u>house warming party.</u>
   그의 친구들이 그에게 집들이를 해주었다.
   ** A party thrown to celebrate when someone moves into a new apartment, flat, or house.

2. He <u>smiled ear to ear</u> when she accepted his dance proposal.
   그녀가 춤추기를 허락하자 그의 입이 귀에 걸렸다.
   ** Have a big smile.

3. He gave his co-workers the <u>cold shoulder.</u>
   그는 동료를 차갑게(냉대) 대했다.
   ** To treat someone in an unfriendly way,

4. <u>Rule of thumb</u>: Don't invite a drunkard to the party.
   경험칙: 술고래는 파티에 초청하지 마시오.

** An approximate method for doing something.

5. Cathy <u>laughed her head off</u> when her rival tripped over her long dress.
   그녀의 라이벌이 드레스에 걸려 쓰러지자 Cathy는 <u>배꼽 빠지게 웃었다.</u>
   ** laugh uncontrollably.

6. She is good at <u>rubbing elbows</u> with her boss at the party.
   그녀는 파티에서 상사와 어울리는 행동을(처세를) 잘한다.
   ** To meet and talk with (someone) in a friendly way.
   [넉살이 좋은 의미]

7. The party pooper <u>cut the rug</u> through the night.
   파티를 망치는 그는 밤새 <u>춤을 췄다.</u>
   ** To dance.

8. He <u>got up the nerve</u> to ask her for a dance.
   그는 <u>용기를 내어</u> 그녀에게 춤을 청했다.
   ** To muster or draw upon one's courage.

9. The tango by invited dancers was the <u>icing on the cake.</u>
   초청한 댄서의 탱고 춤은 그날 파티에 금상첨화였다.
   ** An extra benefit or positive aspect to something already good.

🔍 파티와 카니발 in New Orleans

매년 이른 봄에 루이지애나 주에서 카니발에 오는 사람들은 행렬을 이어 파티를 시작한다.

버본 스트리트(Bourbon street)와 후렌취쿼터(French Quarter) 주위에 술집들이 많고, 술집에서 재즈 밴드 음악과 케젼(Cajun) 음식(gumbo, Jambalaya)을 즐긴다. Covid-19 사건 전 2018년에는 일 년 방문자는 1천850만 명이었다.

〈NOLA〉

Riders will include military veterans from across the United States, firefighters, law enforcement personnel and other public servants. A special Wounded Warriors float will be set aside for Purple Heart recipients, who will ride free of charge. In 2022, the Krewe of Freret welcomed members of the newly formed, all-Female krewe of Them is to its parade lineup.

Themis, which is inspired by The Greek goddess of justice, arose from a controversy within the Mystic of Nyx, which was once arguably the largest Carnival parade.

Authentic Mardi Gras Experience - New Orleans -

BYOB: bring your own bottle party
와인이나 위스키 종류가 너무 많아 파티를 해주는 집에 기본 포도주나 위스키를 제공하고 오는 손님들은 자기기 좋아하는 술은 각자 가지고 오라는 파티. Grab-bag party, slumber party, fare well party…etc.

*** RSVP(répondez s'il vous plaît); please reply.

초대에 참석할지 안 할지 연락주십시오.

Chapter 10.

스포츠

Sports

생활영어 스포츠 1-1

1. The boxer came down from the ring <u>with his tail between his legs.</u>
   그 권투선수는 꼬리를 내리고 링에서 내려왔다.
   ** you feel defeated and ashamed.

2. The tennis player Thomson is <u>over the hill.</u>
   그 테니스 선수 Thomson은 한물갔다.
   ** Describing someone who is old and no longer useful.

3. The athlete couldn't make the <u>final cut</u> for the Olympic team.
   그 선수는 올림픽경기 팀 출전 선수에 발탁되지 못했다.
   ** Final cut: 마지막 선수로 발탁되는 stage.

4. The player <u>took their gloves</u> off from the first round.
   선수들은 1회전부터 격렬하게 싸웠다.
   ** To be aggressive and brutal.

5. Fans face a <u>nail biting wait</u> to hear the umpire's decision.
   관객은 심판의 결정을 들으려 초조하게 만들었다.
   ** Causing great anxiety or tension:

5-2. The Tyson vs Douglas match was a <u>nail biting</u> bout.
   타이슨과 더그라스 경기는 손에 땀을 쥐는 싸움이었다.
   ** Causing intense anxiety or nervousness.

6. The championship game is too <u>close to call</u> regarding who will win.
   그 결승전 경기는 너무 막상막하라 누가 승리할지 모르겠다.
   ** It's too hard to tell who is going to win.

7. The lousy boxer hit his opponent <u>below the belt.</u>
   그 치사한 권투선수가 상대방의 아랫부분을 때렸다.
   ** Unfairly strikes their opponent below the waist.

8. His coach threw in the towel when the boxer got a cut on his forehead.
   권투선수 이마가 찢어지자 그의 코치가 경기를 기권시켰다.
   ** To give up.

9. We won the game against his team hands down.
   그는 경기에서 손쉽게 승리하였다.
   ** To win (something) easily.

10. He will kick your butt if you challenge him.
    자네가 그에게 도전하면 그가 너를 죽사발 만들 거다.
    ** Defeat harshly.

11. We have to face off the strong team again.
    우리 팀은 그 강팀과 다시 대전해야 한다.
    ** To meet an opposing person, group, or sports team to compete.

12. A good seat is hard to come by for $ 100 dollars at the ballpark.
    100불로 좋은 좌석을 경기장에서 찾기는 힘들다.
    ** To find or obtain something, especially accidentally.

13. The ski resort rents basic gear such as ski, gloves, and poles.
    그 스키장은 스키, 장갑, 폴(pole) 같은 기본 장비를 빌려준다.
    ** Equipment.

14. The rafting outfitters supply basic equipment, boat and wetsuits, at the resort in the Grand Canyon.
    그랜드 캐년 리조트에서 기본 장비와 배, 고무 옷을 제공한다.
    Note: 3 day rafting cost was $ 1495 in 2021.

15. The two sprinters finished in a dead heat.
    두 명의 단거리 선수들은 동시에 들어왔다.
    ** A race in which two or more competitors finish at exactly the same time.

Chapter 10. 스포츠 | 77

16. The kid brags he can do 30 push-ups. Fat chance!
    그 아이가 팔굽혀펴기를 30번 한다고 자랑하는데 거의 불가능하다.
    ** Slim or no chance.

17. The bunch of die hard fans tailed gate after their team won the game.
    열열한 팬들은 팀이 승리하고 (주차장에) 모여 축하 뒤풀이를 하였다. [술도 마심.]
    ** Host or attend a social gathering at which an informal meal is served from the back of a parked vehicle, typically in the parking lot of sports stadiums.

18. The players fought up to par even though they were defeated.
    선수들은 패배했지만, 힘껏 싸웠다.
    ** Good as expected or wanted.

19. The power house crushed the opponent.
    그 강팀은 상대방 팀을 박살 냈다.
    ** A strong team.

20. He fought tooth and nail to win the championship.
    그는 챔피언이 되려 악착같이 싸웠다.
    ** With all power or resources being used.

21. Our team never stood a chance against last year's champion.
    우리 팀은 작년 챔피언에게 이길 가능성이 없었다.
    ** To have a possibility. [부정적으로, 가능성이 적다]

22. We all kept our fingers crossed.
    우리 모두는 행운을 빌었다.
    ** Good luck.

Pick the unfit word

A. It is not right if you _____ punch the opponent after a bell rings.
   ① pull ② swing ③ throw ④ veer

B. The team ran out of _____ during the final quarter.
   ① juice ② muscle ③ steam ④ vigor

C. His team'll _____ our poor team again.
   ① bump ② cream ③ lick ④ whip

*** Answer: A-④, B-②, C-①

생활영어 스포츠 1-2

1. The golfer Tiger Woods' 82nd win of PGA Tour game <u>boggled fan's minds</u> in 2022.
   골프선수 타이거 우즈가 2022년 프로골퍼 82번째 승리하자 팬들(fan)은 감탄하였다.
   ** To overwhelm or surprise one.

2. The game was so close that the fans <u>held their breath.</u>
   그 경기는 너무 막상막하라 숨을 죽이고 있었다.
   ** To wait for something specific to happen.

3. He <u>threw a beanball</u> to get even with him.
   그(투수)는 보복하려 타자에게 공을 던졌다.
   ** A pitch aimed at the batter's head.

4. The umpire <u>moved the goal posts</u> in favor of his friend's team.
   그 심판은 자기 친구의 팀을 위해 법을 바꿨다.
   ** To change the rules.

5. The contender has a chip on his shoulder since he was defeated.
   상대방 선수는 그가 전에 패배한 이후 원한을 품고 있다.
   ** Having a grudge against someone.

6. The player's mom was on pins and needles during the penalty kick.
   선수 어머니는 페널티킥 때 바늘방석에 앉았다.
   ** Anxious and tense.

7. The fan believed their team have a game in the bag before the game started in the second-half.
   Fan들은 후반전이 시작하기 전까지 자기 팀이 확실히 이긴다고 믿었다.
   ** Certain to be won.

8. The boxer whistled in the dark until he got up to the ring.
   그 권투선수는 링에 올라가기 전까지 두렵지 않은 척하였다.
   ** Try not to show that you are afraid

9. He felt he is the 5th wheel in his team after his ankle was sprained.
   그가 발목을 삐자 그는 팀에서 필요 없는 선수라고 느꼈다.
   ** Unnecessary person or thing.

10. If he gets smoked next game, he will quit the sport.
    그가 다음경기에 패배하면 운동을 그만둘 것이다.
    ** To be defeated.

11. Fans were wringing their hands while the kicker was ready to kick the penalty kick.
    페널티킥을 차려할 때 응원단들은 조마조마하였다.
    ** To be anxious, worry.

12. Don't gainsay when he shoots the ball.
    그가 공을 찰 때 방해하지 마십시오.
    ** 1) To speak or act against.
       2) To declare not to be true.

13. Fans couldn't <u>make heads or tails</u> who violated the rule first.
    fan들은 누가 먼저 반칙을 했는지 이해할 수 없었다.
    ** fail to understand.

14. The team won the first game <u>by a nose.</u>
    그 팀은 <u>겨우</u> 시합에 이겼다.
    ** Nearly, narrowly.

15. The basketball players joined the <u>point shaving</u> scheme with the gangster to make money at Boston college in.
    1978년 보스톤에서 조폭들의 돈을 벌기 위한 계략에 농구선수들이 참가하여 <u>고의로 점수를 내지 않았다.</u>
    ** the act of a player, or players, doing everything they can to limit how much they score in a game.

16. Some said they were forced to <u>warm the bench</u> because of low grade.
    성적이 나쁜 선수들은 경기중에 벤치에서 (후보로) 앉아있게 하였다고 일부가 말했다.
    ** a reserve player on an athletic team.
    ** bench warmer: 후보선수

Pick an unfit word

A. If you compete with him, he will beat the _____ out of you.
   ① crap ② day-lights ③ hell ④ pipe ⑤ star

B. Two guys'll _____ over the hot babe until one gets knock-down.
   ① bicker ② brawl ③ come to blows ④ slug

** Answer: A-④, B-①

🔍 에베레스트 산 정보

Mt. Everest: 8,848 m. for mountaineers through Nepal.

As of Dec. 2023, 6,664 people have climbed Mt.Everest and reached the summit.

평균 일 년에 35,000명이 등산하러 오지만, 600여 명만 정상까지 올라간다. 대부분은 base camp인 5,400미터까지 올라간다. 추위, 바람, 공기 부족으로 정상을 대부분 기권한다고…

A) Base camp. 5,200 ~ 5,400 Meters.　　B) They wait for good Weather to climb to the top.

A) Once at Everest Base Camp, it then takes an average of 40 days to climb to the peak ofs Mt. Everest.

B) They spend 40 days to adjust and exercise, then to find the right weather to climb to the summit(8,848 m). Base Camp to the summit is 67 miles.

등산객을 위한 정보

적절한 계절: 4월~6월, 9월~11월.
등산 소요기간: 2~3개월.
나이 제한: 18~60세.
입장료: 11,000불.

🔍 정보(Fact)

1. There are hurricane-force winds over 74 mph from October to early April at Mt. Everest.
2. The lowest temperature measured on the summit of Everest was in February 2003 with a -41°C at the summit.
4. At 8,848meter, Everest's summit has approximately one third the air pressure that exists at sea level.
5. At least 35,000 people visit Mount Everest every year.
6. Mt. Everest continues growing every year by at least 4 mm due to the geological uplift.
7. Everest has been well scouted now and there are about 20 routes clearly identified and almost all have been attempted.
8. To date, about 300 people have died.

   ** **Nepal Airport**(Kathmandu) to base camp(5,400m) **and Base camp to the summit is 3,448 m**(8,849m~5,400m)

가격

네팔 공항(Kathmandu)에서 산 중턱(base camp: 5,400m)
15일 가이드 한 명당 $1,500~2,000. 가이드가 몇 명을 요구함.

패키지 가격

네팔 회사(Local outfiter): $25,000~$65,000,
입장료 포함($11,000)
미국회사 RMI 가격 $135,000.
베이스켐프(base camp)에서 에베레스트 정상은 68km.

Chapter 11-1.

여 행

Travel

생활영어 항공

1. We chose the red eye flight to save money.
   돈을 절약하려고 밤 비행기를 선택하였다.

2. Some people get jetlag when they fly more than 3 hours.
   어떤 사람들은 3시간 이상 비행기를 타면 시차를 겪는다.
   ** jetlag: 정신이 멍멍하고 피곤한 멀미.

3. Museum visits are not his cup of tea.
   박물관 방문은 그가 즐겨하는 것이 아니다.
   ** Something one likes.

4. Our group had to play by ear due to the tornado.
   폭풍 때문에 우리 단체는 상황에 따라 행동해야 했다.
   ** 1. To act spontaneously and according to the situation.
      2. Perform a musical piece on an instrument without written music.

5. I hope the rain will go away tomorrow: Knock on wood.
   내일에는 비가 그치기를 희망한다. 좋게 기대해 보자.
   ** To express a hope for one's good luck to continue.

생활영어 비행

1. Passengers get bumped because many airlines are allowed to overbook.
   항공사들이 예약을 정원보다 더 예약을 받게 허가하여 승객들은 비행기를 타지 못했다.
   ** to remove, dismiss, or eject. [no show를 채우려고.]

2. Air fare comes down a bit during the shoulder season.
   성수기와 비수기 기간에는 항공료가 내려갑니다.
   ** 성수기와 비수기 기간.

3. Make his ticket an open return.
   그가 돌아오는 날짜는 미정으로 비행기표를 해주십시오.

4. Please be seated while the airplane is taxing.
   비행기가 이륙하는 동안 좌석에 앉아 있으십시오.
   ** gate에서 활주로에 진입하고 이륙할 때까지 자동차처럼 운전하는 것.

5. If you wish to find your friend, use the courtesy phone.
   공항에서 사람을 찾으려면 공항 내 CP전화를 쓰십시오.
   ** 이 전화는 공항 전체에 방송으로 나가는 무료전화.

6. Page him to meet you at the arrival area C7.
   도착하는 (1층) C7에서 (공항 내 스피커로) 그에게 당신을 만나자고 방송하십시오.
   ** 1층에서 승객이 내리고 2층에서 탑승함.

7. Report the missing luggage at the lost & found.
   못 찾은 가방을 분실물 보관소에 신고하십시오.

8. You just have 2 hours of layover time, hurry up.
   비행기를 바꿔 탈 때 걸리는 연결 시간이 2시간 있으니 서둘러야 합니다.
   ** 비행기를 바꿔 탈 때 (연결) 주어진 시간.

9. Don't forget to declare if you have more than 10 thousand dollars.
   만 불 이상의 돈이 있으면 신고하는 것을 잊지 마십시오.

10. The custom agent arrested a passenger for smuggling contraband.
    세관원은 금수품을 밀수하는 승객을 체포하였다.
    ** goods that are prohibited by law from being exported or imported
       illegally imported or exported goods.

생활영어 여행

1. We have 4 pieces of luggages to check (to send).
   부칠 가방이 4개 있습니다.

2. Can I see your valid passport?
   유효한 여권을 보여 주십시오.

3. Get the boarding pass at the ticket counter.
   탑승권은 항공권 발행하는 곳에서 받으십시오.

4. Put me on the Waiting list for an economy ticket.
   나를 일반석 대기명단에 올려주십시오.

5. Arrival time on the ticket is local time.
   비행기표의 도착 시각은 현지 시각입니다.

6. Black-out days mean that airlines don't sell cheap tickets during the long holiday.
   긴 휴일 때는 항공사가 저렴한 항공권을 발행하지 않는 기간입니다.
   ** Black-out-days 의미는 항공사가 크리스마스, 연말 공휴일 때에는 저렴한 항공표를 팔지 않는 기간을 의미.

7. Put the carry-on luggages in the overhead bin.
   가방(carry-on)은 머리 위 수납함에 넣으십시오.

8. Put the seat-back in an up-right position while taking off or landing.
   이륙과 착륙 시 의자의 등받이를 90도 위치로 올려 주십시오.

🔍 항공여행에 대한 정보

Open Jar

LA에서 출발하여 NYC에 가고, NYC에서 Boston을 방문하고, 다시 NYC에 돌아와 비행기를 탈 필요가 없이 Boston에서 LA로 탑승하게 해주는 제도. 가고 돌아올 때 거리가 같으면 허락해주는 제도.

Drop off charge

rental car를 운전하기 시작한 곳과 차를 돌려주는 장소가 다르면 돈을 받는데, extra charge가 없는 회사가 있다.

🔍 항공기 내에서 준수할 정보를 영어로 들으려면

https://www.youtube.com/watch?v=0ldFV_JGyKM

유럽 기차 패스 가격

https://www.interrailguide.com
7일 패스: 성인(28~59 yrs) $568, 청소년(12~27yrs) $456.
10일 패스: 성인 $699, 청소년 $ 561.

여행정보

여행정보를 BBC, PBS에서 찾았는데 이제 Youtube에서 DW(독일) 공영방송을 찾는다. 제공하는 인터넷은 경치뿐 아니라 사회, 풍습,경제, 역사 같은 정보도 들을 수 있다. 영국의 BBC, 독일의 DW, 미국의 PBS 국영방송을 추천.

추가 정보

Europe: Rick Steves or Ryan Shirley.
Scandinavia(북유럽): Scenic Hunter, Eva Z. Beck.
China: Ryan Shirley, Brad.
Norh America: CCRT travelers,

BBC-travel Journalist Kate Humble: 좋은 정보.
Napal, Mongolia, Siberia, Afcanistan, India, Congo
DW: The Russians- An intimate journey through Russia.

Grand Canyon

A) 1~18 days @ Grand Canyon
협곡 콜로라도 강. 래프팅 Rafting.

B) Supai 마을에 사는 인디언
Havasupai 족에게 우편을 배달.

길이(Length): 446km, 깊이(Depth): 1,400m~3,000m.

A) There are more than a dozen of outfitters in Las Vegas, Arizona State, Utah State, and Indian Tribe nation.
B) Mules carry mails to Havasupai Hava indian village, Monday to Friday. It is a 9 miles walk one way.

Mules have been carrying mail and goods to the Havasupai people located Inside the Grand Canyon. 10-22 mules are used daily, along with one wrangler on horseback, 5 days a week, traveling 9 miles down into the canyon to the Supai Post Office.

Grand Canyon Mail by Mule - Grand Canyon Questions

그랜드-케넌 협곡 아래 흐르는 코로라도 강 주위에 사는 마을을 관광하려면 헬리콥터 tour나 mule tour가 있고 원주민이 1883년 자주 국가가 되고 일부 주위에서 여행, 식당들을 원주민들이 운영하고 있다. 그랜드-케넌을 따라 흐르는 코로라도 강에서 1일~18일 래프팅(rafting)은 라스베이거스, 애리조나, 유타 주, 그리고 미국 원주민들이 운영하는 투어가 4지역, 더구나 도시마다 만든 투어 가격과 옵션(option)들이 다양하여 가격을 잘 조사하시길. 이 Grand Canyon 협곡은 Lake Mead(Las Vegas, NV)에서 시작하여 Lake Powell(near Page, Arizona)까지 446km 길어서 (white Water Rafting) 출발지점이 다르며, 가격은 하루에 $399불에서 18일은 $ 7,000불까지이다.

** 개장기일: 3월 15일~10월 31일.
** 래프팅: 한여름을 피하고 봄, 가을을 택하시길.
** 3days- $1490, 6days- $5,500, 18days-$ 7,000. Arizona, Utah, Nevada 3주에서 운영하여 가격이 많이 차이가 있으니 조심하길.

Grand Canyon West is situated on the Hualapai Indian Reservation and is an enterprise of the Hualapai Tribal Nation, a sovereign Indian nation that has been federally recognized since 1883. The tribe doesn't receive federal funding for the operations at Grand Canyon West. Every purchase at Grand Canyon West helps to sustain Hualapai the tribe's capital is Supai. The population is 639.

Tourism is a large portion of the economy of the reservation. The tribe runs its own tourism office as well as a café, lodge, and general stores.

여행객들이 많이 찾는 도시

1	Rome, Italy	21.0 million
2	Istanbul, Turkey	20.2 million
3	Tokyo, Japan	19.5 million
4	London, UK	18.8 million
5	switzerland	18.5 million
6	Paris, France	15.5 million
7	Bangkok	15.2 million
8	Berlin, Germany	12.1 million
9	N.Y. City, USA	11.7 million
10	Barcelona, Spain	7.8 spain

**Las Vegas, 40.8 million.
** Most Las Vegas tourists are not on vacation. But they visit there for business conventions.

🔍 겨울 휴가 휴양지

Islands	From Miami(Mile)	낮-밤. Jan.
Key West (Usa)	1,163	24 / 17℃
Bahama (Nassau)	1,154	25 / 20℃
Jamaica-(Ocho Rios)	1,554	29 / 23℃
Cosco Rico- San Jose	1,101	26 / 18℃
Caribbean Side	1,150	31 / 21℃
St. Thomas	1,104	28 / 22℃
Cancun-Mexico From Lax	2,108	24 / 22℃

1월 기온

뉴욕시- 영하 4도(최하~18도).
보스톤- 영하 6도(최하~19도)
시카고- 영하 8도(최하 영하 26도) Latitude : 41.5 N.

보스톤, 뉴욕, 시카고 지역 주민들은 겨울인 1월이 되면 추위를 피하려고 카리브의(caribbean), 멕시코로 휴가를 받아 떠난다.

마이애미에서 500마일 아래쪽 자메이카 지역 바닷물은 화씨 75도가 넘어 스노크링을 1시간 이상 해도 춥지가 않고, 1,000마일 남쪽 코스타리카까지 내려가면 바닷물이 화씨 80도(26.6c)가 넘어 온천물 같아 두세 시간 스노크링을 할 수 있다.

키 웨스트(Key West, FL)에는 해삼이 많고, **Bahama**에서 세인 토마스(St. Thomas)에는 어른 주먹만 한 소라(conch), 자메이카에서는 성게를 북부 해변에서 잡을 수 있다.

Blue Sea @ Mosquito Bay in Vieques

Mosquito Bay in Puerto Rico

A) 바닷물에 자라는 미생물이
물체에 닿으면 빛을 만든다.

B) Mosquito Bay in Puerto Rico에 미생물
dinoflagellates가 파도로 밤에 파란 빛을 만듬

마이애미에서 1,014마일 남쪽 섬. San Juan 공항에서 버스로 2.5시간, 서남쪽 해변에 미생물이 많이 산다. 바다에 살고 있는 미생물(dinoflagellates)이 다른 물질이나 파도에 닿으면 빛을 발한다. 손을 대거나 배가 지나가면 파란 불을 만든다.

Blue Light at nigh

Some plankton in the sea make light when we touch the sea water. When I touched the sea water, it lit up. It turns so bright when the wind is strong.

Mosquito Bay, Puerto Rico

Recognized in 2006 by Guinness World Records as the Brightest Bioluminescent bay in the world, Mosquito Bay Vieques captivates with its beauty and pristine setting. … The bay's mesmerizing brightness is due to the large concentration of dinoflagellates – a quantity that was hurricane inexplicably doubled after María – ranging from an average of 1,000,000 to 2,100,000 per gallon of water.

미국 입국 시 금지품목

미국 입국 시에 소시지, 육포, 장조림, 만두 등 육류성분이 들어 있는 식품류와 과일, 씨앗, 쌀, 콩, 벗기지 않은 마늘, 뿌리가 남아 있는 자연상태의 농산물.

Chapter 11-2.

여행(교통)

철도(Amtrak), 버스(Greyhound)

생활영어 운송1-1

1. Take the belt-way to avoid traffic jams.
   복잡한 교통을 피하려면 외곽도로를 타세요.
   ** A highway that encircles an urban area so that traffic does not have to pass through the center.

2. The bus was jam-packed like sardines by passengers.
   버스에 승객들로 버스가 콩나물 시루처럼 빽빽했다.

3. Two car drivers are bitterly fighting over a fender bender.
   두 운전사는 경미한 접촉사고로 격하게 싸우고있다.
   ** The vehicles involved are only slightly damaged.

4. Lucky us, at least, we have liability car insurance.
   적어도 책임보험이라도 있으니 우리는 다행임.

5. Don't park the car on the shoulder lane. It's a towing zone.
   갓길에 차를 세워놓지 마십시오. 견인 지역입니다.

6. We drove at break-neck speed to catch the train.
   기차를 타려고 (차를) 빠른 속력으로 운전하였다.
   ** Very fast.

7. His mom, backseat driver, chews his ear off if he drives fast.
   말로 뒷좌석에서 운전하는 그의 어머니는 그가 운전을 빨리 하면 그의 귀가 따겁게 잔소리한다.
   ** Passenger in a car who gives the driver unwanted advice.

8. The driver turned right on the spur of the moment to avoid on-coming car.
   운전사는 접근하는 차를 피하려 순간에 우회전을 하였다.
   **Without planning or thinking careful

9. His big sister draws her eyebrows while she is behind the wheel.
   그의 누나는 운전하면서 눈썹을 그린다.
   **Driving a motor vehicle.

10. The motorcycle gang is tail-gating us.
    모터싸이클 깡패들이 우리 뒤를 바짝 뒤에서 쫓아온다.
    ** Drive too closely behind (another vehicle).

11. Call him when you are in the neck of the woods.
    당신이 그의 집 근처에 가면 그에게 전화하시오.
    ** Area where someone lives.

12. Step on it. We have got to catch the train.
    밟아라(accelerator). 그 기차를 타야 한다.

13. The Mustang Picks up speed fast, accelerating from 0 to 60 miles per hour in just 3.3 seconds.
    머스탱 차는 (처음 출발 시) 3초에 60마일 속도를 올린다.
    ** 속도를 올리다(accelerate).

생활영어 운송1-2

1. The bus was stalled in the middle of nowhere.
   그 버스는 아무도 없는 외딴곳에서 시동이 꺼졌다.
   ** To stop.

2. The street is a towing zone after sun-down.
   해가 진 이후에는 그 길은 (자동차) 견인지역이 된다.

3. The two cars had a deadly head on collision.
   두 자동차가 무서운 정면충돌 하였다.
   ** Meeting with the fronts or heads foremost directly.

4. Wheel alignment increases mpg and life of the tires.
   휠 정렬은 자동차 바퀴 수명이 길어지고 연비(mpg)가 높아진다.
   ** Wheel alignment: 차체와 바퀴를 나란히 맞춤.

5. She luckily found a helper to give a jump.
   여성은 운좋게 충전을 도와주는 사람을 찾았다.
   ** To force electricity through the dead car battery. [To start the car]

6. The cop pulled us over to give us a ticket.
   경찰은 (교통위반) 딱지를 주려고 우리를 도로 옆에 세웠다.
   ** Move a car to the side of or off the road.

7. Pull up to the Pick up window for your hamburger order.
   햄버거를 찾으려 돈 내는 창문으로 몰고 오십시오.
   ** To drive (a vehicle) to a specific place.

8. The punk blew the red light again.
   그 건달은 또 빨간불을 지나갔다.
   ** To pass through an intersection despite it is a red light without stopping.

9. The selfish driver suddenly cut into our lane.
   얌체가 갑자기 우리 줄 앞에 끼어들었다.
   ** Move quickly in front of another car.

10. The suspect was arrested in a hit and run.
    차를 박고 뺑소니친 범인은 체포되었다.
    ** Crime where a perpetrator does something (car accident) and leaves the scene as quickly as possible.

11. The inbound traffic is bumper to bumper every morning.
    시내로 들어가는 교통은 매일 아침마다 차가 밀린다.
    ** 복잡한, 차가 밀리는. ** outbound: 시외로 향한

12. U.S. Highways that run east/west are even numbers(2, 4, 6, 80).
    미국 고속도로 숫자가 짝수이면 동서로 가는 길이다.
    ** 홀수를 가진 고속도로는 남북으로 가는 고속도로이다.

🔍 Give me a break(한번 봐주십시오)

1. Officer! Give me a break. I won't pass the red light.
   경찰아저씨! 빨간불에 건너가지 않겠으니 한번 봐주세요.

2. He said he can pull up 30 times. Give me a break. [과장]
   그가 턱걸이를 30번 할 수 있다고 말했다. 좀 봐주라.

3. Don't deny you broke my bike. Give me a break! [거짓말]
   자네가 내 자전거를 부순 것을 부인하지 말게. 좀 봐주라.

   ** DMV: 미국 운전면허시험장(Department of Motor Vehicles)
   LA, Chicago, NYC, ATL에서는 한글로 면허시험 볼 수 있습니다.

🔍 미국 횡단 기차 & 버스 요금

〈뉴욕시- Los Angeles〉 거리: 3,935km.
〈기차〉 Amtrak 소요시간: 81시간(NYC~LA)
요금: One Way- $137~315.
침대차(Roomette): $ 3,924. 한 방에 2명의 왕복표값.
한 방에 침대 2개, 화장실1, 3식을 5.5일간 제공.

기차 시간 & 요금

Travel Guide to Train Fares – Easy Online Booking Options | Amtrak

버스

Greyhound Bus: one way.
소요시간: 66시간.
요금(one way): $ 150~230.

🔍 미국횡단 여행정보

NYC~Denver까지는 평야라 옥수수, 밀, 목장들이 대부분임.
덴버에서 LA 사이에 산이 나타나고 대여섯 개의 국립공원이 있음.

🔍 국립공원

Utah State: Zion, Bryce, Arches National Park.
Grand Canyon: Arizona, Utha,
Yellowstone: Wyoming, Montana, Idaho
Rocky Mountain-Denver, Colorado.

*** Union Station: 미국 도시 중앙 기차 정거장 이름.
*** Note: 서울역을 설명할 때 기차는 Seoul train station보다 Seoul Central Train Station이라고 해야 외국인들이 이해하기 쉽다. 서울에 기차 정거장이 청량리, 용산역도 있으니….

Chapter 12.
전 화

Phone Phrase

이제 전화를 하면 사무실에서 녹음된 문장으로 질문하는 경우가 대부분이라 발음이 정확하지 않으면 기계가 계속 묻다가 대답하는 발음을 하지 않은 것으로 인식하고 끊어 진다. 아래 문장 같은 대화나 질문의 Answering Service 녹음을 듣고 발음 연습을 잘 하시기를. 아래 Site에 여러 답하고 질문하는 문장이 있으니 연습하시기를.

아래에 한 여성의 대화에 여러가지 경우로 구분해 놓았음.

https://www.speakconfidentenglish.com/telephone-calls-in-english/

간단한 문장 번역을 참조하십시오.

1. Her phone rings off the hook Friday afternoon.
   금요일 오후가 되면 그 여성의 전화통이 불이 난다.

2. Press the phone number followed by the pound key.
   전화번호를 누르고 나서 우물 정 자를 누르십시오.

3. Press area code first if it is a long distance call.
   장거리 전화라면 지역번호를 누르십시오.

4. Your call will be answered according to its place in the order of calls we have received.
   우리는 전화를 받은 순서대로 전화를 받겠습니다.
   [전화를 받는 녹음된 기계가 말하는 첫 말입니다.]

생활영어 전화-basic

** May I ask who is calling?
전화 하시는 분이 누구신가요?

** Please hold on a minute(or please hang on).
잠깐 기다리십시오.

** I will connect to him.
그 남자에게 연결해드리겠습니다.

** He is out of his office.
그가 잠깐 사무실을 비웠습니다.

** She is on the other phone(or line) now.
그 여성은 지금 다른 전화로 통화 중입니다.

** May I take a message?
메시지를 받아 놓을까요?

** Put him on. It's an emergency.
그를 바꿔주세요. 긴급한 일입니다.

** Call him before the store closes.
가게 문닫기 전 그에게 전화하십시오.

** Pick up the phone(or Answer the phone, please).
전화 받으십시오.

** May I put you on hold(or Hang on please).
전화를 (끊지 말고) 잠시 기다리시겠습니까?

　　** 800 numbers: 수신자가 지불하는 전화번호
　　** Collect Call: 전화하는 사람이 받는 사람에게 지불하게 하는 전화 [전화국 직원 통해서]
　　** 911: 한국에서 119와 같은 전화 [긴급 시 사용]

Chapter 13.
건강 & 의학

Health & Medicine

🔍 미국 내 10대 좋은 병원

Mayo clinic. Rochester, MN.
Cleveland clinic, Ohio St.
UCLA Medical Center. Los Angeles.
John Hopkin Hosp. Baltimore.
Massachusetts General Hosp. Boston
Cedar- Sinai Medical Center, Los Angeles.
New York-Presbyterian Hosp. NYC.
NYU Langone Hosp. NYC.
Barnes-Jewish Hosp. St. Louis.
Brigham and Women's Hosp. Boston.

위의 병원이나 Clinic은 선정된 병원이니, 의문이나 질문이 있으면 이 병원이나 Clinic의 정보를 찾으면 더 믿을 만한 정보나 의학지식을 찾을 수 있습니다.

생활영어 의학1-1

1. The family breathed <u>sigh of relief</u> when they found the surgery was successful.
   수술이 성공적이라 식구들은 <u>안도의 한숨</u>을 쉬었다.
   ** A feeling or display of relief.

2. The biopsy result turned out to be a <u>malignant tumor.</u>
   그 조직검사 결과는 <u>악성 종양</u>으로 나타났다.

3. The male doctor made the pregnant woman <u>ill at ease</u> during the regular check-up.
   그 남자 의사 정규 검진은 임산부를 <u>불편하게</u> 만들었다.
   ** Disturbed, awkward.

4. Entire world has been trying to <u>ward off</u> the Covid-19.
   전 세계는 코로나 병을 <u>퇴치하려고</u> 하고 있다.
   ** Repel, drive back.

5. The doctor found polyps at the big colon through the Colonoscope.
   의사는 내시경으로 대장에서 용종을 발견하였다.
   ** A colonoscope is a long, thin, flexible instrument that is inserted into the anus for a visual inspection of the colon and rectum.

6. The patient's autopsy turned out to reveal a malignant tumor.
   그 환자의 조직검사는 악성 종양으로 나타났다.

7. The poor thing is under the weather while her mom is in hospital.
   어머니가 입원한 동안 저 불쌍한 것이 좀 아프다.
   ** Feeling slightly sick.

8. Omega-3 has been shown to help lower triglycerides or blood fats.
   오메가 3는 피속에 기름, 나쁜 지방질을 낮게 해준다.
   ** Triglycerides are a type of fat.

9. The neighbor's hearts went out to the kid when his mom was admitted in hospital due to cancer.
   아이의 엄마가 암으로 입원하자 이웃의 동정심이 발했다.
   ** Feeling great sympathy for somebody.

10. The world has been trying to keep the Corona virus at bay.
    전 세계는 코로나바이러스를 멀리하려고 하였다.
    ** To keep someone or something at a distance.

11. There is no silver bullet for toe nail fungus.
    발톱에 곰팡이를 (퇴치할) 특별한 치료제가 없다.
    ** A simple remedy for a difficult problem.

생활영어 의학1-2

1. You can buy pain-killers <u>over the counter</u> in the US.
   처방전(prescription) 없이 진통제를 미국에서 살 수 있다.
   ** Sold lawfully without prescription.

2. Diabetes is a <u>chronic disease</u> causing many other illnesses.
   당뇨병은 다른 병을 유발시키는 만성질환이다.
   ** continuing or occurring again and again for a long time.

3. Apply <u>antibiotic ointment</u> on a cut after cleaning it with antiseptic to prevent infection.
   염증을 막으려면 찢어진 상처를 살균제(알코올)로 항생제 연고를 바르십시오.

4. The doctor decides a patient's admission and <u>discharge.</u>
   환자의 입원과 퇴원은 의사가 결정한다.

5. Nurses tend <u>around the clock</u> at the intensive care unit.
   중환자실에는 간호사가 24시간 지켜있습니다.
   ** Entire 24-hour day.

6. Grammar school kids often <u>come down with</u> a cold in the winter.
   초등학생들은 겨울이면 자주 감기에 걸린다.
   ** Begin to suffer from a specified illness.

7. Give <u>booster shots</u> to kids before starting to attend grammar school.
   초등학교 입학하려면 아이들에게 예방주사를 맞히세요.
   ** A supplementary dose of an immunizing agent administered as an injection.

8. The <u>primary doctor</u> suggested the patient get a referral to a specialist for his heart surgery.
   주치의는 환자의 폐수술을 위한 전문의 소개를 제안하였다.
   ** Directing someone to another person, usually someone with more specific expertise, for further action.

9. **Inflammation** between his gum and his cavities gives him unbearable pain.
   잇몸과 충치 사이의 염증은 그에게 참기 힘든 고통을 준다.

10. Cold can be <u>transmitted</u> by a sneeze.
    재채기로 감기는 옮겨질 수 있다.
    ** To pass or cause to go from one place or person to another.

11. Wash the vegetables and fruits thoroughly. Those might be <u>contaminated</u> with pesticides and weed killers.
    채소와 과일들은 제충제와 제초제로 오염되어 잘 씻어야 한다.

12. Color blindness runs in his family.
    색맹은 그 집의 유전이다.
    ** Common in a family; passed down from ancestors.

13. Malnourished people are <u>vulnerable</u> to germs.
    영양실조에 걸린 사람들은 세균에 약하다.
    ** Capable of or susceptible to being attacked, damaged or hurt more so than usual.

14. Infant <u>mortality</u> in Africa is astoundingly high.
    아프리카 유아 사망률은 놀랄 만큼 높다.
    ** The state of being subject to death.

15. White blood cells play a key role in <u>innate</u> immunity.
    백혈구(피)는 병을 막는 데 중요하게 타고난 면역 역할을 한다.
    ** Resistant to a particular infection.

Pick an unfit words

A. The _____ of the bird flu killed 51 people and 40 Millions of chickens in Vietnam in the 2,000s.
  ① discord ② epidemic ③ outbreak ④ pandemic

B. Exercise _____ endorphins that makes people happy.
  ① provides ② releases ③ secretes ④ stirs

*** Answer : A-①, B-④

🔍 소비자들이 인터넷에서 받을 의학정보

2022년 미국에 6,120 병원이 있으며, 다섯개 별 받은 병원은 483개 (12.6%)라고 CMS가 보도. You Tube에 기업이나 상인들이 돈 욕심에 너무 많은 정보가 과장되거나 거짓 정보가 나타난다. 위에 추천한 10개 병원이나 Clinic은 선정된 병원이니 의학에 관한 의문이나 질문이 있으면 이 병원이나 Clinic의 정보를 찾으면 더 믿을 만한 정보나 의학지식을 찾을 수 있습니다.

Important health information on Internet or youtube sometimes are not accurate, sometimes wrong. If you wish to know reliabel infs, check with the hospital data in the Youtube.

🔍 제약회사의 범죄- Sackler family-Purdue Co.

중독되는 진통제를 20여 년 생산해온 회사 Purdue의 소유자 Sackler 가족이 중법으로 판결을 받고 문을 닿았다. 의사의 처방전 없이도 매입할 수 있는 마약이 섞인 진통제를 팔아온 그 가족 때문에 20여만 명이 사망하여 $8 billion을 배상 판결받았다. 한국의 가습기로 몇명이 사망했을가? 살균제 사망으로 SK, 애경 기업들의 배상과 책임이 궁금하다.

🔍 제약회사 Purdue의 범죄 by U.S. Dept. of Justice

"Purdue admitted that it marketed and sold its dangerous opioid products to healthcare providers, even though it had reason to believe those providers were diverting them to abusers," Attorney for the United States Rachael A. Honig, District of New Jersey, said. "The company lied to the Drug Enforcement Administration about steps it had taken to prevent such diversion, fraudulently increasing the amount of its products it was permitted to sell. Purdue also paid kickbacks to providers to encourage them to prescribe even more of its products."

District of New Jersey |
Opioid Manufacturer Purdue Pharma Admits Guilt in Fraud and Kickback Conspiracies |
United States Department of Justice

Chapter 14.
인종차별 & 계급사회

Racism & Class Society

Ms Parks refused to give in her front seat to White people

She joined Dr. Martin King Jr. for anti-discrimination in 1955.

생활영어 인종차별

1. India has its own ranking of <u>Varna</u> system. However, in every region, the Dalits are at the bottom of the hierarchy and over the centuries.
   인도는 지역마다 그들의 <u>사회계급제도</u>가 있으며, Dalit 계급은 수백 년간 제일 낮은 계급이다.
   ** A system of persons or things ranked one above another.

2. The Dalit community have also performed tasks such as manual <u>scavenging</u>, the inhumane practice of removing human waste both hand from sewers from birth.
   (인도의 최하급) D 계급은 <u>버린 물건을 주워먹고</u> 태어날 때부터 하수구에서 오물을 맨손으로 제거하는 천한 일을 해왔다.
   **To take or gather (something usable) from discarded material.

3. One Japanese male moved to a remote village to get married. He was a butcher in his home-town where his village people would <u>disdain</u> his job in the 1980s.
   1980s년 한 일본 남자는 결혼하려고 외딴 마을로 이사하였다. 그때 마을 사람들이 백정을 <u>천대하였다.</u>
   ** To look down.

4. APA said that the denial of structural racism was linked to anti black prejudice.
   조직적인 인종차별을 부인함은 반흑인 편견에 연관되어 있었다고 심리학 협회가 말했다.
   ** an unreasoned and unfair distortion of judgment in favor of or against a person or thing.
   APA: The American Psychological Association(심리학 협회)

5. Racism and antipathy towards Southeast Asians is unfortunately quite common among Koreans.
   동남아시아계 인종차별과 경멸은 한국인들 중에 꽤 많이 있다고 한다.
   ** A strong feeling of dislike.

> 🔍 1955년 흑인 여성이 백인의 앞좌석에 앉아 체포되었다.

백인들만 앉는 버스 앞 좌석에 흑인 여성 Ms. Parks은 앞좌석에 앉고 백인 승객에게 좌석을 양보하지 않았다고, 1955년 12월 1일 몽고메리(Alabama 주) 경찰에 체포되고 흑인단체 NAACP와 함께 평등운동을 위해 거리로 나섰다. 2015년에는 흑인교회 7곳이 Charlotte, N.C. 주위에서 10일 사이 화재가 발생하였다. 백인 우월단체 KKK의 공격이었다. 심지어 1970's 중순에도 Chicago(Sheridan bus lane) 버스 앞좌석에는 백인들이 앉고 흑인, 유색인들은 뒷좌석에 앉았다.

> 🔍 Library of Congress in USA

When Rosa Parks was arrested on December 1, 1955, for refusing to give up her bus seat to a white man, she was mentally prepared for the moment.

Earlier that summer, she attended a workshop on implementing integration at the Highlander Folk School in Monteagle, Tennessee.

Also at that time, the Montgomery NAACP had been looking for a test case to challenge the constitutionality of Alabama state bus segregation laws. To coincide with her trial on December 5 in 1955, the Women's Political Council initiated a one-day citywide bus boycott.

The Bus Boycott | Explore | Rosa Parks: In Her Own

Words | Exhibitions at the Library of Congress
| Library of Congress (loc.gov)

🔍 Against discrimination 〈Stanford University〉

Parks inspired tens of thousands of black citizens to boycott the Montgomery city buses for over a year. During that period she served as a dispatcher to coordinate rides for…

https://kinginstitute.stanford.edu/parks-rosa

🔍 Baptist Press 백인 우월주의자, KKK.

백인 우월자들(KKK)은 2000년 초 미국 남부지역 South Carolina에서 7개의 흑인 교회에 방화하였다,

The latest fire destroyed Mt. Zion African Methodist Episcopal Church in the small town of Greeleyville, S.C. The church had been rebuilt after the Ku Klux Klan burned it to the ground 20 years ago.

Greeleyville is 65 miles north of Charleston, the site of the massacre at Emanuel AME Church that took the lives of the pastor, leaders and others ranging in age from 26~87 as they were praying in Bible study. Arson was confirmed in a June 24 fire that caused $250,000 in damage at Briar Creek Road Baptist Church in Charlotte, N.C., a predominantly black Southern Baptist church that also hosts services for two Nepali congregations.

7 black churches burned in 10 days | Baptist Press

Chapter 15.

공 해

Pollution

🔍 세계 대도시 공해 인덱스(INDEX)- 미세먼지(PM2.5) in 2023.

(**두 번째 숫자는 공해가 가장 심한 계절의 수치)

New Delhi, India: 92.2(?),
Beijing, China: 34.1(53.9),
Seoul, Korea: 19.7(29.9),
New York city: 11.6(16.8),
Paris, France: 10.3(17.8),
Los Angeles: USA .9.5(6.0),
London, England: 8.4(12.0),

Hanoi, Vietnam: 43.7(?)
Hong Kong: 27.0(?)
Rome, Italy: 13.1(22.70)
Moscow, Russia: 10.4(13.1)
Berlin, Germany: 10.5(13.6)
Tokyo, Japan: 9.1(10.3)
Honolulu: 4.9(?)

생활영어 공해

1. Cars <u>emit</u> toxic carbon dioxide through an exhaust pipe.
   자동차는 배기관으로 독한 이산화탄소를 <u>배출한다.</u>

2. <u>Inhalation</u> of CO_2 damages a human's lung, causing <u>respiratory failure.</u>
   이산화탄소를 흡입하면 사람의 폐를 손상시키며 호흡에 큰 장해를 일으킨다.
   ** The action of inhaling or breathing in Respiratory serving for or functioning in respiration.

3. California Law bans schools locating less than 500 feet from highway because of car <u>fumes.</u>
   캘리포니아 법은 자동차 매연 때문에 학교가 고속도로에서 500피트(152 미터) 이내에 위치할 수 없게 금지시켰다.
   ** Smoke in the exhaust emissions of a motor vehicle.

4. <u>Untreated</u> Industrial waste and chemical fertilizers flow into rivers and oceans.
   깨끗이 처리하지 않은 공장의 폐기물이나 화학비료는 강이나 바다로 흘러들어간다.
   **Not treated with a reagent or dye, or not subjected to chemical or physical treatment.

5. Gas from coal and cars, carrying carbon dioxide and other gas, become a greenhouse around the earth, keeping the temperature hot.
   석탄과 자동차에서 나오는 매연인 이산화탄소(CO_2)와 gas가 지구를 온실처럼 둘러싸서 고온을 유지시킨다.

6. Japan said they will release 1.27 million gallons of contaminated radioactive water into the ocean in 2023 after they treat it.
   일본은 2023년 방사성 물질로 오염된 1백27만 갤론의 물을 처리하고(정수) 바다로 방류시킨다고 말했다.
   ** Tainted with unhealthy materials.

7. In 2021, people gathered in Knoxville to commemorate 200 some workers who are sick or died after cleaning toxic coal ash that spilled in Kingston, Tennessee in 2008.
   2006년 킹스톤-테네시 주에서 (둑이 터져) 흘러내린 석탄재를 청소했던 사람 200여 명이 사망하거나 병에 걸린 유족을 추모하려고 2021년 낙스빌에 모였다.
   ** 저수지처럼 석탄재를 저장한 둑이 무너너졌다.

8. Coal ash commonly contains some of the earth's deadliest lethal materials such as lead, mercury, arsenic, cadmium.
   석탄재는 일반적으로 인간에게 아주 치명적인 납, 수은 같은 물질이 섞여있다.
   ** Deadly.

9. Insecticides kill bees and butterflies that pollinate flowers of fruit plants.
   살충제는 유실수의 꽃가루를 수정시켜 주는 벌이나 나비를 살해한다.
   ** Insect killer.

10. Plastic waste in our oceans harm many life forms, disrupting the delicate balance of the marine ecosystem.
    해중에 있는 버린 프라스틱은 여러 바다의 생명들을 해치며, 섬세한 이코 시스템의 바란스를 교란시킨다.
    ** To throw into confusion or disorder.

11. The scientists recommend that they should release it slowly to dilute it with the ocean water for a 10 years period of time.
    학자들은 (방사성으로 오염된) 물을 희석시키기 위해 10여 년간 천천히 바닷물과 섞어 흘려보내야 한다고 추천하였다.

****Make** (a liquid) thinner or weaker by adding water.

12. **Asbestos** is used as an insulator to keep out the cold and retain heat. But it causes lung cancer.
    석면은 방열제로 사용하는데, 암을 유발한다.

13. Korean cement makers brought Japanese coal ashes in Korea as a **dumping** site. And Koreans took money from Japan.
    한국의 시멘트 공장은 일본의 석탄재를 버리는 매립장처럼 한국에 들여왔다. 그리고 일본에게서 돈을 받았다.

14. Heavy flood in summer makes river and sea coast polluted by run-off.
    여름마다 대홍수가 넘쳐 흘러 강과 해변을 오염시킨다.
    ** Flow over and away from a surface

🔍 일본 핵발전소 사고

〈UN News〉 Nuclear Accident in Japan.

WEB Aug 24, 2023 · The decision to release the water into the sea has sparked criticism in Japan and the region. Long-term commitment. The IAEA has been providing real-time data on the controlled release of the treated water, including on water flow rates and radiation monstoring.

"The IAEA has committed to be present before, during and after this process…"

핵폐기물을 40년간 정수하고 바다에 희석시켜 방류한다고 말한다. 누가 40년간을 감시하고 지켜볼까?

일본 후꾸시마의 핵발소 사건 이후 독일은 핵발전소 긴설을 중지하겠다고 정부가 발표하였다.

🔍 Green Peace

WEB Aug 22, 2023 · "We are deeply disappointed and outraged by the Japanese Government's announcement to release water containing radioactive substances into the ocean. Despite concerns raised by fishermen, citizens, Fukushima residents, and the international community, especially in the Pacific region and neighboring countries, this decision has…

🔍 AP News

WEB Aug 22, 2023 · Members of environmental civic groups hold signs during a rally to denounce the Japanese govern ment's decision to release treated radioactive water into the sea from the damaged Fukushima nuclear power plant, outside of a building which houses Japanese Embassy, in Seoul, South Korea, Tuesday, Aug. 22, 2023.

🔍 CNN

WEB Aug 23, 2023 · An aerial view of the Fukushima plant after the start of the release of treated radioactive wastewater in Japan on August 24, 2023. ... Japan's devastating 2011 earthquake and tsunami caused ...

China bans all seafood from Japan after release of treated radioactive …

🔍 Los Angeles school Decision on Pollution

L.A.는 2003년 학교가 고속도로 500 feet 이내로 학교를 건설 못 하게 법을 통과시켰다.
미세먼지(2023년): 한국- 19.7, L.A.- 9.5

2003 state law prohibits schools from being built within 500 feet of major roadways unless the district can mitigate the pollution or space limitations leave it no option.

L.A. Times.

Chapter 16.

종 교

Religion

🔍 성당 St. Boniface Church in San Francisco에서

노숙자들을 교회에서 재워주는 교회

A. 노숙자를 재워주는 교회 @ SFO. Running a Food Bank too.

B. St. Boniface Church in San Francisco for the homeless.

생활영어 종교

1. The church has been providing a <u>shelter</u> for the Homeless in San Francisco for the past 15 years.
   B 천주교는 지난 15년간 도시(SFO)에서 노숙자에게 거처할(밤에 잠잘 곳을) 제공해 주었다.
   ** Something that covers or affords protection.

2. The Boniface catholic church has been a <u>beacon</u> of home for the homeless people in San Francisco.
   그 B 교회는 sfo 노숙자들에게 등불이 되어 주었다.
   ** A light or fire that acts as a warning or signal.

3. Providence Baptist church in the city <u>followed suit</u>, providing a sleeping place for the homeless nightly.
   P. 침례교회는 B 교회를 따라서 밤에는 노숙자에게 교회를 제공해 주었다.
   ** Imitate or do as someone else has done.

4. One church has been providing <u>pews</u> for 120 mothers and Children during the freezing winter time.
   한 교회는 120명의 어머니와 아이들에게 추운 겨울 교회의 긴 의자를 제공하였다.

** Long bench(resting place)

5. Minister Jo, Yong-Gi of Soon-Bok-Eum church in Seoul, the biggest church in Korea, was <u>behind bars</u> for a few year due to the misuse of church money.
한국에서 제일 큰 교회인 서울의 순복음교회 조용기 목사는 교회 돈을 불법으로 사용하여 교도소에 있었다.
** In jail or prison

🔍 성당 St. Boniface Church in San Francisco

노숙자들을 성당에서 재워주는 교회

미국 샌프란시스코의 천주교 St. Boniface 성당은 추운 겨울 노숙자들을 성당에서 재워주고 식사도 제공하기 시작하였다.
이 지역 여러 교화는 이렇게 노숙자들을 돕고 있다.
Guests pull blankets tightly around them, covering feet and hands cracked and dry from the cold.
For a few hours they rest and a decent sleep, something that living on the street rarely provided.
Today they can find refuge in a place that welcomes them. They can stretch out on benches and rest.
Except where they sleep is not on benches but on pews in St. Boniface Church in San Francisco.
···The image is striking Boniface Church— a city's homeless population asleep on church pews, finding sanctuary in a church's nave.
 This program at St. Boniface is part of the Gubbio Project, which provides blankets, hygiene kits, and socks to around 150 people who rest in the church each Weekdays.

지정환 신부: Catholic priest Didier t'Serstevens

A) 지정환 신부님. 24세부터 시골에 거주하며 농민을 위해 농토를 개간하며, 가난한 서민을 위해 치즈 공장을 세워주다가 88에 사망하였다.

B) 유신헌법에 항거하다 1970s에 체포당했다.

지정환 신부는 벨기에서 태어나시고 1959년에 한국에 정착하자, 가난한 시골농민 에게 개척한 농토를 농민에 나누어 주고 치즈 공장을 만들어 마을에 기증하였다. 1970s애는 군사독재 정치의 유신헌법을 반대하다 체포되었다. 학생 위한 장학회를 설립하시고 신부님이 정년퇴직 하시고, 노년에는 노인 치료에 기여하다가 88세에 한국에서 사망하셨다.

Belgian-born Catholic father came to Boosan, Korea in Dec. 1959. Since then, he had been devoting his entire life for hungry poor Korean farmers. While serving as a priest, father cultivated $300,000$ pung(평) reclamation land, and gave $9,927 m^2$ farm land to 100 village farmers. In 1964, he built a cheese factory to assist starving families in Im-sil, Chun-Buk. He went back to Belgium to learn about cheese making skills. And he got support from his family in 1967.

When he returned from Europe, most workers disappeared with his cattles. Later, he donated the cheese factory to the village co-op. While he had been running it successfully, In the middle of 1970s, he was arrested due to a protest against a military dictator who changed a law(유신헌법) to be a permanent president.

Later the father set up a health care center for handicap people in Jun-Ju area in 1984. One year later, he accepted Korean Citizenship from the Korean government. After he stepped down as a priest in 2004, father found a scholarship institution, calling "Rainbow House", for students in need in 2007.

Until his final day, at a secluded village, he had been working for more than 100 handicapped people for 20 some years. The father passed away on Apr.13, 2019, at the age of 88.

He was buried In Jun-Ju city in Korea.

🔍 메시아라고 자칭하던 사이비 목사 짐 존스

자신이 메시아라 하던 Jones 목사는 미국이 자기 교인들을 박해하여 천국의 유토피아를 만들겠다고 SFO에서 남미(Guyana)로 교회와 교인들을 옮겼다.

학대 비리로 의심받던 Jones의 사실을 발견한 후 언론사 기자와 Ryan 하원의원이 조사하러 방문하려고 떠나자, 사이비 목사는 박해하는 세상을 떠나자고 1978년 교인들에게 독약을(cyanide) 주스에(Kool Aid) 넣어 마시게 하여 918명이 사망하였다.

🔍 BBC-TV

WEB Nov 18, 2018 · More than 300 children were killed in the 18 November 1978 massacre... Jones simultaneously urged his more than 900 followers to take their own lives, warning that the Guyanese military would... Nov. 17, 2018.

Jonestown: Rebuilding my life after surviving the massacre (bbc.com)

🔍 Britannica

WEB Jun 26, 2024 · Jim Jones (born May 13, 1931, Crete, near Lynn, Indiana, U.S.— died November 18, 1978, Jonestown, Guyana) was an American cult leader who promised his followers a utopia in the jungles of South America after proclaiming himself messiah of the Peoples Temple, a San Francisco-based evangelist group. He ultimately led his followers.

Jim Jones | Biography, Jonestown, Massacre, Peoples Temple, & Facts | Britannica

According to Guyana escapee Teri Buford O'Shea, once the Peoples Temple moved down to South America, Jones made followers believe that the military was after them. He told them that American soldiers were waiting in the woods to kill anyone who ventured too far away from the compound.

🔍 Ranker

O'Shea told The Atlantic, "We didn't know this at the time, but he'd set up people who would shoot into the jungle to make us feel as if We were under attack. And there were other people who were set up to run and get shot - with rubber bullets, though we didn't know it at the time. So there you were, in the middle of the jungle. Shots were being fired and people were surrounding you with guns."

15 Horrific Tactics Jim Jones Used To Keep His Followers On Lockdown (ranker.com).

Chapter 17-1.

언론 TV & 예술

+ Sinclair Broadcaster

생활영어 언론

1. As the Capitol riot unfolded on Jan. 6. the reporter <u>fabricated</u> the peaceful demonstration.
   1월6일, 국회의사당 폭동을 평화로운 궐기라고 그 기자는 사실을 조작하였다.
   ** To make up for the purpose of deception
   ** The Capital: 국회의사당

2. Most of foreign news stations display English <u>subtitle</u> on TV In the USA.
   미국에서 대부분의 외국 뉴스는 TV 화면에 영어로 번역된 자막을 보여준다.
   ** Secondary or explanatory title see more noun of foreign dialogue of a movie or TV program.

3. Two candidates appeared for a <u>grip and grin</u> after a heated debate.
   두 명의 출마자들은 열띤 논쟁 후 사진 찍으러(선거용) 나타났다.
   ** A photo where people shake hands and smile at the camera.

4. The magazine's cover story is about a criminal <u>anecdote</u>.
   그 잡지의 표지 스토리는 범죄조직에 대한 짧은 글이다.
   ** A short story, tale.

5. The radio DJ took a <u>payola</u> from a mediocre singer for playing a song of her new album.
   라디오 DJ는 시시한 가수의 새 앨범의 노래를 틀어주고 뇌물을 받았다.
   ** The practice of paying bribes or graft for commercial advantage or special favors.

6. The weekly magazine will cover a special <u>feature</u> on electric cars.
   그 주간지 잡지는 전기차에 대한 특별기고를 다룰 것이다.
   ** A newspaper or magazine article or a broadcast program devoted to the treatment of a particular topic.

7. The paparazzi's photo was sold $ 80 K to the magazine.

   그 사진기자(파파라치)의 사진은 잡지사에 8만 불에 팔렸다.

   ** Independent photographers who take pictures of high-profile people; such as actors, musicians, athletes, politicians, and other celebrities.

8. Facebook with 45,000 employs is a huge SNS followed by Twitter in the USA.

   45,000명 직원을 가진 인터넷 방송 Facebook은 트위터보다 크다.

   ** social networking service.

9. Now-a-days, major US news media use round-ups for their news.

   근래에 큰 언론사들은 짧은 뉴스를 모은 것을 뉴스에 많이 사용한다.

   ** Collection of short news or stories.

10. Concerned Americans worried when Tabloid and Youtube spread biased news and unproven information.

    타블로이드와 youtube에 편견적인 뉴스와 증명되지 않은 정보가 퍼져나가서 미국인들이 걱정하고 있다.

    ** A tabloid is a newspaper, especially one that's smaller than a traditional daily paper and focuses on sensational news items.

    흥미 위주의 신문.

11. On the contrary, it is an exaggerated parody.

    그 글은 (본작품과) 반대로 과장되어 쓴 글이었다.

    ** A humorous or satirical imitation of a serious piece of literature or writing.

🔍 Sinclair 언론사 기업

　이 미국 언론사는 전국에 193 언론사를 소유하고 있으며, 미국 정치에 공화당을 지원하는 언론사 기업이다.

　Fox 언론사와 함께 깊이 정치에 개입한 언론사이며 MSNBC, CNN은 민주당을 지원하는 언론사들이다. CBS, NBC, ABC TV 언론사와 미국의 Washington Post, New York Times 신문사들은 미국에 큰 언론사들이다. 국영방송으로는 NPR, PBS TV이다.

미국 대기업 언론사들의 정치개입

Sinclair broadcast group

By NPR 라디오.

Sinclair, based in suburban Baltimore, owns and controls more than 190 stations across the country. Sinclair has a long tradition of Republican ties on and off the air over time, it hired two ex-Trump administration aides, one as a commentator, another as a lobbyist.And Pai swept away decades-old inhibitions against greater consolidation in the local television industry— something that he had discussed with Sinclair chairman. David Smith just before Trump elevated Pai to lead the FCC. May, 2020- NPR.

FCC Hits Sinclair With Record Fine For Deception In Bid For Stations : NPR

Chapter 17-2.

연예 & TV

Entertainment & TV

생활영어 연예

1. Williams' joke knocked fan' socks off on the NBC Carson show.
   윌리엄의 농담은 NBC의 C 쇼에서 대단한 인상을 주었다.
   ** Impress someone in a very strong and way.

2. His joke is cut and dried.
   그의 농담은 흥미가 없다.
   ** Uninteresting.

3. Tim's comedic gesture brought down the house.
   Tim의 (노망한 역) 코믹한 연기에 (관객의 웃음으로) hall이 떠나갔다.
   ** To cause the audience to erupt in applause.

4. The audience rolled in the aisles when Robin said jokes at the NBC show.
   NBC 쇼에 로빈이 농담을 하자 관객이 웃어 죽었다.
   ** Laughing uncontrollably.

5. Will smacked Chris right after Chris pulled a punch line at Oscar.
   C가 오스카 시상식에서 W(의 부인)에게 결정타의 농담을 한 후 W는 C에게 주먹질을 하였다.
   ** Final part of the typical joke structure.

6. He was depressed even though his mistake was for the bird.
   그의 실수는 별것이 아닌데도 그는 아주 낙심하였다.
   ** Unimportant.

7. Didn't we just hear that song playing? Wow! Real radio déjà vu.
   우리들이 저 노래 연주한 것 다시 들었던 거 같은데?
   와! 라디오에서 나타난 '데자뷔'인데.
   ** The feeling that you have already experienced something that is happening.

8. Many TV executives push the envelope to increase viewers ratings with sexy and violent programs.
   시청률을 올려 TV 간부들은 난폭하고 성적인 프로를 더 첨가하려고 도를 넘게 밀어부친다.
   ** Exceed the limits of what is normally done.

9. Undeveloped nations' news media overuse sound-bites that neglect a citizen's basic rights.
   저개발 국가들의 언론은 시민들의 기본권리를 등한시하고 눈에 잘 띄는 글을 너무 사용한다.
   ** Catchy statement that is easy remember.

10. His off the cuff remark was awkward at the interview on the gun restriction issue.
    그의 총기 제재 문제에 대한 인터뷰에서 준비 없는 그의 논평은 어색하였다.
    ** Without preparation.

11. Some of US television shows are dubbed into Spanish for Mexican viewers.
    일부 미국 TV쇼는 방송할 때 멕시코 시청자를 위해 스페인어를 (자막에) 삽입한다.
    ** To change or add the sounds and speech on a film or TV.
    (동영상이나 영화에 음악이나 글을(subtitle) 첨가.

12. The music publisher is toying with a medley of the beatles hit.
    그 레코드 출판사는 비틀스의 오래된 히트곡 노래 전집을 다시 만들 생각을 하고 있다.
    ** A musical composition consisting of a series of songs or other musical pieces from various sources.
    ** Toy wIth: to thInk about.

생활영어 언론

1. The <u>caption</u> will explain how the car was overturned.
   그 <u>사진의 설명</u>은 차가 어떻게 전복됐는지를 말해줄 것이다.
   ** A title or explanation for a picture.

2. The producer rejected your article's title because it was <u>cliché</u>.
   당신의 글 제목은 너무 <u>진부한 것</u>이라고 제작자는 (쓰기를) 거절하였다. [불란서 단어 크리쉐]
   ** Expression that was once innovative but has lost its novelty due to overuse.

3. Exhausted by all of the <u>hoopla</u>, the singer was glad to see the curtain closing.
   (관객들의) 환성에 지친 가수는 커튼이 닫히자 기뻐했다.
   ** Noise and activity in celebration of an event.

4. His jokes <u>fell flat</u> at the TV show
   TV쇼에서 그의 농담은 <u>완전히 실패였다</u>.
   ** To be completely unsuccessful.

5. PBS will <u>simulcast</u> the State of the Union with NPR.
   (국영방송) PBS는 NPR 라디오와 (대통령) 연두교서를 <u>동시방영</u> 할 것이다.
   **Simultaneous transmission of the same program on radio and television.

6. Mr. Kimmel has a <u>knack</u> for entertaining NBC talk shows.
   K 씨는 NBC-TV쇼를 운영할 재주를 가지고있다.
   ** Natural skill at doing something.

7. The movie "Avengers" was a <u>block-buster</u> in 2019.
   2019년 영화 "에번져"는 <u>대박</u>을 터트렸다.
   ** Big hit.

8. The kid goes movie to get <u>early bird</u> discount on Saturday.
   조조할인을 받으려 토요일 첫 상영 영화를 보러 간다.
   ** 대부분 첫 상영.

9. Avatar has become the first film in history to pass $2.9 billion at the global box office.

영화 "아바타"는 세계 영화관람 판매액이 역사상 처음으로 $29억 불이 넘었다.

** a place at a theater or other arts establishment where tickets are bought or reserved.

영화 관객으로 수입이 있고, 또 영화로 생기는 장난감 t-shirts 같은 부수입.
"Box-office"는 관객 수입.

Connect related words

A. chick   1. comedy
B. slap   2. flick
C. stand-up   3. jerker
D. soap   4. opera
E. tear   5. stick

*** Answer: A-②, B-⑤, C-①, D-④, E-③

ABC TV 연속 코메디, All in the Family

1971~1979년 Emmy 상을 22번 받은 연재 코메디로 ABC-TV가 미국 사회에 큰 영향을 준 쇼라고 주간지 Atlantic이 평하였다. 아이리시(Irish) 장인이 같이 사는 폴란드 사위를 놀리고 무시하는 코메디 작품이다. "미국에서 폴란드 사람들이 머리가 나쁘다고 놀린다." 신랄한 비판을 받을 사회의 문제점을 잘 그렸다. 한국애도 이런 좋은 작품이 많이 나오기를.

"All in the Family" is touted as the series that brought reality to prime-time TV entertainment. The lead character, Archie Bunker, is a loudmouthed, uneducated bigot who believes in every stere-type he has ever heard. His wife, Edith, is sweet but not the sharpest knife in the drawer. They and their daughter, Gloria, and her husband, Mike, all live in a working-class home. Unfortunately for Archie, he can't avoid the people he disdains: His son-in-law whom Archie calls "Meathead" -- is an unemployed student and of Polish descent…

⟨By Rotten Tomato⟩

All in the Family condensed the "generation gap" of the 1960s Into a single living room. It pitted Mike Stivic, a long-haired liberal, and his wife, the bubbly Gloria, against Gloria's father, Archie Bunker, a reactionary bigot and Richard Nixon–dockworker—as Edith, the daffy but benevolent wife and mother, looked on. Incarnated by a stellar cast and energized by brilliant writing and directing, it became a television landmark, widely lauded as one of the greatest and most influential shows ever.

⟨The Atlantic⟩

Chapter 17-3.

예술

Art

생활영어 예술

1. The new rock group <u>took the town by storm.</u>
   새로운 록 그룹은 그 도시에서 큰 인기를 얻었다.
   ** Make a vivid impression on, quickly win popular acclaim.

2. The gorgeous back-up dancers <u>stole</u> the singer' <u>show.</u>
   뒤에서 춤추는 멋진 댄서들이 가수의 인기를 빼앗았다.
   ** They get a lot of attention or praise(taking attention from else).
   After the violin student said he can play Zigeunerweiser, He has no choice but to <u>face the music</u> when the teacher Picked him to Play at the school festival.
   그 바이올린 배우는 학생이 Z곡을 연주할 수 있다고 말하자, 선생님은 그 학생이 (능력이 없는데도 힘든) 곡을 학교 패스티벌에 연주하게 시켰다.
   [실력 없는 사람이 큰소리치고 대표처럼 무대에 선 case]
   ** To accept the unpleasant results of an action. to be ready to accept punishment. 말 실수로 고통받는 의미.

4. The candidate for the chorus singer is a bit <u>tone deaf.</u>
   합창단 가수 지원자는 약간 음치이다.
   ** Unable to distinguish differences in musical pitch.

5. To be a concert pianist was his <u>pipe dream.</u>
   그가 콘서트 피아니스트가 된다는 건 헛된 꿈이었다.
   ** An unattainable hope or plan.

생활영어 음악

1. The <u>lyrics</u> of Richard Strauss's 'Four Last Song' are poem of Herman Hesse.
   리차드 스트라우스 마지막 4곡의 가사는 헤르만 헷세의 시(詩)이다.

2. Pianist Moors had <u>accompanied</u> many prominent singers.
   피아니스트 무어 씨는 저명한 성악가에게 반주를 해주었다.
   ** Play a musical accompaniment.

3. Every orchestra members <u>tunes</u> to the oboe's A note before they perform.
   오케스트라의 단원들은 연주하기 전에 오보 악기의 A음(라)에 맞추어 조율한다.
   ** To adjust an instrument to a desired pitch or key.

4. Ave Maria is the <u>signature song</u> of Schubert who wrote 140 songs in his prime time.
   슈베르트의 전성기에 작곡한 140곡 중 대표할 곡은(18번) 아베마리아 곡이다.
   ** most closely identified with or best known song. 18번

5. The pianist <u>interpreted</u> the song "Reverie" that Debussy wrote to express his daydream.
   그 피아니스트는 드뷔시가 꿈(몽상)을 묘사하려고 작곡한 Reverie 곡을 잘 표현하였다.
   ** To represent by means of art.

6. Beethoven's lieder are Northern Europeans <u>gente</u> for solo singers.
   베토벤 작곡의 lieder 곡은 북유럽 지역의 솔로 성악가들이 부르는 성악곡 종류이다.
   ** Gente(장르): a particular style, form of art works or music.

7. 'Trout' <u>quintet</u> was composed by Schubert when he was Just 22 yrs old.
   송어 오중주 곡은 슈베르트가 단지 22세 때 작곡하였다.
   ** A group of five people playing music or singing together.

8. The back up singers sang with the tenor at the <u>refrain.</u>
   후렴에서는 back-up 가수들이 테너와 함께 노래하였다.
   ** a short succession of notes producing a single impression.

9. He played the song <u>by ear</u> on the piano without music note after he heard the song a few times
   그는 그 노래를 두어 번 듣고 <u>악보 없이</u> 그 노래를 피아노로 쳤다.
   ** To play a piece of music without referencing sheet music

10. Ms. Sutherland showed her best <u>rendition</u> when she sang the version of "Casta Diva."
    소프라노 서더렌드가 카스타 디바를 노래할 때 그녀의 <u>표현</u>은 최상이었다.
    ** a performance or interpretation, especially of a dramatic role.

11. The director made a <u>song and dance</u> when a reporter Questioned why he chose a disqualified singer for the opera casting.
    오페라 배역에 자격 없는 가수를 선택했느냐고 기자가 질문하자, 그 감독은 <u>헛수작</u>을 하였다.
    ** A misleading statement, nonsense.

12. The painter's <u>guild</u> increased the member's fees 5% to enlarge the archive size for their art works.
    미술인 <u>협회</u>는 그들의 예술작품 저장을 확장하려고 회비를 5% 올렸다.

시(詩)와 노래(Lied) By Hermann H esse

작곡가: Richard C. Strauss
가사(詩): Hermann Hesse.
소프라노: Jessi Norman

R. Strauss: Vier letzte Lieder, TrV 296 – 4. Im Abendrot (youtube.com)

노래 제목: At Sunset(Im Abendrot)
Lyrics(English Translation)

We have gone through sorrow and joy hand in hand;
Now we can rest from our wandering above the quiet land.
Around us, the valleys bow; the air is growing darker.
Just two skylarks soar upwards dreamily into the fragrant air.
Come close to me, and let them flutter.
Soon it will be time for sleep.
Let us not lose our way in this solitude.
Oh vast, tranquil peace,
so deep at sunset!
How weary we are of wandering...
Is this perhaps death?

** 작곡가 스트라우스는 1948년 그가 84세에 4곡을 작곡하였다.

1. Spring(Frühling)
2. September
3. Going to sleep(Beim Schlafengehen)
4. At Sunset(Im Abendrot)

Srauss's Four Last Songs are simply one of the most touchingly beautiful ways for a composer to end his career, says Jane Jones. At the end of a long and successful career, when a composer still has the power to move.

🔍 lip sync 설명

가수들이 큰 광장이나 운동장에서 노래를 부르면 관객들이 잘 듣지 못하여 레코드를 틀어주고 가수가 입만 벌려 직접 부르는 것 같이 보여준다.

🔍 Public Domain

작가의 작품을 타인이 사용 못 하지만 70년이 지나면 그 작품을 사용할 수 있다.

Consists of all the creative work to which no exclusive intellectual property rights apply. Those rights may have expired, been forfeited, expressly waived, or may be inapplicable. Because no one holds the exclusive rights, anyone can legally use.

Chapter 17-4.

종합 예술

Silk Road Project

Along the Silk Road by Yo Yo Ma.

서기 600여 년부터 아시아에서 지중해까지 왕래하던 Silk Road 주변 20여 국가들의 예술을 모아 Yo Yo Ma가 1998년 음악단체를 만들었다. [Silk Road 주변국]

China, Mongolia, Korea, Uzbekistan, Tajikistan, Azerbaijan, Iran, Turkey

🔍 YoYo Ma' Silk Road Project

The SILK ROAD PROJECT is a nonprofit arts and educational organization with a vision of connecting the world's neighborhoods by bringing together artists and audiences around the globe. Founded by cellist Yo-Yo Ma in 1998 as catalyst to promote innovation and learning through the arts, the Silk Road Project takes inspiration from the historic Silk Road trading routes as a modern metaphor for multicultural and inter disciplinary exchange.

The SILK ROAD ENSEMBLE is a collective of internationally renowned performers and composers from more than 20 Countries. Each Ensemble member's career to one of the preeminent artistic challenges of our times: to maintain the integrity of art rooted in authentic traditions while nourishing Global connections.

Many of the musicians first came together under the artistic direction of Yo-Yo Ma at a workshop at Tanglewood Music Center in Massachusetts in 2000. Yo-Yo Ma serves as the artistic director of the Silk Road Project. He is also a creative consultant to the Chicago Symphony Orchestra, a member of the President's the Arts and Humanities, and a recipient of the 2010 Presidential Medal of Freedom.

The Silk Road Ensemble with Yo-Yo Ma | LA Phil

He uncovers Asian Music

🔍 Yo Yo Ma's wonderful Project

Flash Mob

2003년 즈음, 여러 예술인들이 큰 광장에서 모여 음악이나 무용을 발표하기 시작하였다. 많을 때는 12,000명, 대부분 넓은 기차 정거장, shopping mall에서 음악가들이나 무용하는 예술인들이 발표한다. 명문 음대 (Juilliard)를 졸업해도 한정된 오케스트라 단원에 선정되기 무척 힘든 현실이라 관객이 많이 참석할 수 있는 곳에서 연주하는 기회는 사회에게 예술을 전달할 수 있는 좋은 기회이다. Good Luck Folks.

large groups of people who suddenly assemble in a public place, perform an unusual act, such as dances or playing music, then quickly disperse—captivated the public imagination in the early 2000s. While flash mobs are less common today than during their peak from 2003~2011. The first flash mobs were created in Manhattan in 2003, by Bill Wasik, senior editor of Harper's Magazine.

Grease – Central Station Antwerp – YouTube@ Antwerp, Belgium.
Beethoven Flashmob Mensa Heidelberg #HDFlashmob – YouTube @ Heidelberg.

Chapter 18-1.

경폐 + ESOP

Economy and ESOP

생활영어 경제1-1

1. The president had to bail out GM to save it from bankruptcy.
   대통령은 파산하는 GM 회사를 구해주어야 했다.
   ** To help, save.

2. It's on the verge of economic collapse due to the irresponsible US banking industry in 2008.
   무책임한 은행 때문에 2008년 (미국은) 경제 붕괴 순간에 처했다.
   ** The moment of break-down.

3. Many stores scrambled to borrow money to pay rent during the Covid-19 pandemic.
   코비드-19 사태로 많은 가게들은 집세를 내기 위해 돈을 빌리려 허겁지겁하였다.
   ** To struggle frantically in order to get something.

4. The U.S. economy hit rock bottom in 2008. The change of monetary policy was too late in 2008.
   2008년에 금융정책 수정이 너무 늦어서 경제가 바닥을 쳤다.
   ** To reach the lowest point.

5. The U.S. government lowered interest rates to get out of the bear market.
   미국 정부는 경제 침체에서 벗어나려고 이자를 낮추었다.
   ** Slow economy.

6. European Union were in same boat when the recession hit the USA.
   미국이 경제 침체가 오자 유럽연합도 처지가 같았지.
   ** In the same difficult situation.

7. The bank of Japan kept its benchmark rate at virtually 0% from 0.75% in 1999 to 2,000.
   1999~2000년 일본은행은 기준 이자를 0.75%에서 0%로 낮추어 이자를 주지 않았다.
   ** To measure according to specified standards.

8. They hope the economic stimulus package is <u>a shot in the arm</u> for the country's recession.
   국가 경제 침체를 위해 경제회복(정책) 패키지는 경제를 <u>고무시키는(자극)</u> 정책이 되기를 희망하고 있다.
   ** Boost, encouragement,

9. In the end, what it all <u>boils down to</u> is money.
   결국 모든 것은 돈이다.
   ** To summarize, to make a long story short.

10. After <u>crunching numbers,</u> they decided not to buy a RV. (recreation vehicle)
    계산을 해본 후 캠핑카(rv)를 사지 않기로 하였다.
    ** To analyze numbers or exams.

11. Stevens, Alaska senator, proposed to build a bridge, a typical "<u>White Elephant</u>" for 50 some Island people with $ 398 million tax dollars.
    알래스카 국회의원 스티븐슨은 50명 섬 사람을 위해 <u>허울 좋은 것</u>(다리)을 건설한다고 3억 9,800만 불 세금을 쓸 제의를 하였다.
    ** A big item is troublesome or useless.

12. With the cold weather and the high cost of heating fuel, home owners get hit with a <u>double whammy</u> this winter.
    추운 기후로 비싼 겨울 연료비 때문에 집소유자들은 이번 겨울에 <u>두 가지로 고통</u>을 받는다.
    ** A situation that is bad in two different ways.

13. It seems the stock price may be <u>bottoming out</u> next spring.
    증권 가격이 내년 봄에 <u>바닥을 칠 것</u> 같다.
    ** To reach the lowest point.

14. His family are <u>scraping by</u> on minimum wage in the village.
    그의 가족은 마을에서 최저임금으로 <u>근근이 살아간다.</u>
    ** To live with barely enough money.

15. A report on 300 top US companies found CEOs making an average $ 10,6 million with the median workers getting only $23,968(The Guardian June 7, 2022).

미국 직원들은 평균 $ 23,968을 받는데, 300개 미국 대기업의 회장들은 평균 $10.6 millions불을 받는다고 보도하였다.

** Median income: 인구 중 제일 많은 직원들이 받는 월급.

Pick an incorrect word

A. The dark cloud is _____ over Japan's economy in early 2,000.
① clinging ② hovering ③ lingering ④ looming

B. The stock market _____ in 2009, hitting the lowest ever.
① fell ② plummet ③ plunged ④ sprout

C. The US market has been _____ with TV sets coming from all over the world.
① flooded ② inundate ③ saturated ④ swept

D. The oil price has been _____ from $2.50 two years ago to $ 7 dollars in 2022, calf.
① skyrocketed ② smeared ③ soared ④ surged.

E. The renewable energy company will _____ with the government aid.
① flourish ② prosper ③ recoil ④ thrive

*** Answer: A-①, B-④, C-④, D-②, E-③

생활영어 경제1-2

1. China's huge gas consumption will have a huge <u>ripple effect</u> in the world economy.
   중국의 많은 정유 소비는 세계경제에 <u>여파</u>가 클 것이다.
   ** A situation in which one event produces effects which spread and produce further effects.

2. The Wall Street <u>put their ear to ground</u> to find the Fed's interest rate change.
   증권가는 정부의 이자율 변동을 알아보려 <u>경청한다.</u>
   ** To listen for any indication of what is happening.

3. His family <u>bet his shirt</u> to buy a lithium mine in Nevada.
   그 가족은 네바다에 있는 L 광산을 사려고 <u>위험하게 큰 투자를 하였다.</u>
   ** To bet or risk everything one has on some wager or venture.

4. The government subsidy for the car industry did not <u>make a dent</u> in the nation.
   자동차 생산공장에 대한 정부지원은 (미국경제에) <u>큰 도움이 되지</u> 못하였다.
   ** To show initial progress or impact.

5. Citi-Group's surprise profit: Are banks really <u>out of the woods.</u>
   시티은행의 놀라운 이익(증가): 그 은행들은 <u>곤경에서</u> 벗어났을까?
   ** Out of a difficult situation.

6. The Shanty town people have been living from paycheck to paycheck, the <u>vicious cycle</u> under the free enterprise system.
   자유경제 조직에서도 그 달동네 사람들은 <u>악순환</u>으로 근근히 살아왔다.
   ** Negative series of events that build on and reinforce each other.
   ** Shanty town: 가난한 동네
   ** Live paycheck to paycheck: 봉급으로 겨우 산다.

7. Some are in a <u>rat race</u> to drive a Lamborghini in a fast lane.
   어떤 사람들은 람보르기니 (고급)차를 (소유하고) 운전하려고 빠른 차선(경쟁)에 끼어서 <u>바쁜 생활의 경쟁에</u>

끼어든다.
** Fierce competition for success, wealth, or power.

8. Driving a car to work place is <u>double edged sword</u> when you have a difficult time finding a parking spot at downtown.
   직장에 차를 가지고 다니는 것은 장·단점이 있다. 중심가 주차할 곳을 찾는 일이 힘들다.
   ** Something that has or can have both favorable and unfavorable consequences.

9. Every cloud has a <u>silver lining.</u>
   구름 변두리에는 희망이(햇빛이) 보인다.
   (쥐구멍에도 볕 들 날 있다는 의미와 비슷)
   ** A good situation can be followed by something bad or negative.

10. His 20 years' hard work <u>went up in smoke.</u>
    20년 힘들게 해온 일은 다 <u>날아가버렸다.</u>
    ** Come to nothing, be shattered, be ruined.

11-A〉 The investors see a <u>light at the end of the tunnel.</u>
    그 투자자들은 터널 끝에 희망이(햇빛) 보인다.
  B〉 The light at the end of the tunnel is on-coming train head light.
    터널 끝에 보이는 불빛은 굴속으로 들어오는 기차 불빛이다.
    ** 변형: 희망이 아니고 재앙이 온다.

12. A〉 The <u>bottom line</u> is that recycling isn't profitable.
    결론으로 (말하면) 재활용(사업)은 이익이 나지 않는다.
  B〉 The <u>bottom line</u> is, he's gone and he's not coming back
    결론으로 말하면 그는 떠났고, 다시 돌아오지 않는다.
    ** the final total of an account, balance sheet.

🔍 미국의 새 경제정책: ESOP

이 기업조직이 평직원에게도 도움이 되는 기업을 만들기 위해 직원들이 기업의 주식을 매입하여 기업에 주주가 되어, 기업의 간부만 특권을 갖지 말고 평직원도 참정권을 받아 51%가 되면 회장, 간부들의 특권을 직원들이 감시할 수 있는 제도이다.

Here are some key points.

ESOP grants company stock to employees, often based on the duration of their employment. Shares vest over period of time.ESOP is used by employers to reward employees or as an exit strategy from business ownerShip. ESOP shares are part of employees' remuneration for work performed. Employees with ESOPs become potential shareholders and can buy stock options.

🔍 Princeton University report

In the first quarter of 2024, 67 percent of the total wealth in the United States was owned by the top 10 percent of earners. In comparison, the lowest 50 percent of earners only owned 0.5%6 of the total wealth.

Top Wealth in America: New Estimates under Heterogeneous Returns – Princeton University – Department of Economics

ESOP is a program that allows employees to become partial owners of the company they work for by acquiring shares of the company's stock. Devendra S. Neegi- Forbe.

ESOP(Employee Stock Ownership Plan) is a retirement plan that provides employees with an ownership interest in the company12345.

🔍 Harvard University

Ever since 1974, when Congress enacted the first of a series of tax measures designed to encourage employee stock ownership plans (ESOPs), the number of employee-owned (or partially owned) companies has grown from about 1,600 to 8,100, and the number of employees owning stock has jumped from 250,000 to more than eight million.

The Big Benefits of Employee Ownership(hbr.org)

Chapter 18-2.
한국 경제

The South Korean Economy

부패한 한국 독재자들이 70여 년간 형성한 한국의 가족 재벌.
경제를 만들고 현 정치가들이 개정을 하지 않고 있다.

BBC Apr. 24, 2017

Samsung, Lotte, LG, Hyundai: they are unavoidable, selling everything from mobiles to laptops, cars to washing machines as well as food, drink and even health insurance. Staggeringly, sales revenue from the top five chaebols are worth more than half of South Korea's entire economy.

Is real reform possible at South Korea's chaebols? - BBC News

윤석열 정부의 추경호씨가 경제를 살린다고 2023년 한국 경제의 68% GNP를 차지한 10개 가족 재벌에게 세금을 22%로 낮게 해주었다. 정경유착의 한 예이다. 한국의 건물주들은 입주자에게 주택가격의 70%~80%를 전세라는 이름으로 받는다. 한국만 존재하는 특혜를 주었다. 미국에서는 집 소유자들은 3개월 월세를 보증금(security deposit)이라고 세입자들에게 받고 있다고 Zillow 회사가 보도하였다. 대기업들이 금융업인 증권사와 보험기업까지 소유하게 허락하여 중소 기업들은 한국경제 발전을 지연시키고 있다. 대한항공이 아시아 항공을 소유하고, 현대는 미국시장에 단 한 기업의 독점(MONOPOLY)인데, 일본은 8개 회사가 있다.

미국에 수출하는 일본 8개 자동차 회사

Toyota, Honda, Nissan, Mazeda, Subaru, Mitsubishi, Daihatsu, Mitsuoka, Isuzu. <Motorcycle>: Suzuki, Yamaha

인도가 식민지에서 벗어난 지 80년이 가까워지는데 이제 167명의 억만장자는 있어도 비정규 직원들은 80%이며, 일용직 하루 임금이 4.6불이라는 NPR 기사가 있었다. 이제 한국의 고통받는 중소기업은 한국 대기업 위한 정경유착에 기대할 수 있나?

<Harvard Article>
Park Chung-hee, who was president from 1963 to 1979. His policies enabled the chaebols' success through government contracts, legislative support and financial benefits; in return, he demanded that chaebol leaders adhere to his…

Franchise royalty fees list - Google Search Esop(Employee stock ownership)

한국 같은 가족 재벌이 큰 경제 파워를 가진 국가에서는 직원들이 기업의 주식 51% 소유하여 직원들의 권익을 가질 수 있는 제도를 미국에서 만들었다.

Chapter 18-3.

기업 운영

Business Practice

Conspiracy by GM, Standard Oil & Fire Stone

생활영어 기업 운영1-1

1. Steve started to build Apple computers in his garage on a Shoe-string budget for which he sold his VW car in 1976.
   스티브는 VW 자동차를 판 소액의 돈으로 차고에서 1976년 Apple 컴퓨터를 만들기 시작하였다.
   ** Very small sum.

2. Steve Jobs made the most important computer marble in the world with his high school friend.
   스티브는 그의 고등학교 친구와 세계에서 가장 귀중한 것인 컴퓨터를 제작하였다.
   ** Wonderful thing or work of art.

3. The CEO lowered the break-even point as a last resort.
   그 회장은 최후의 수단으로 손익분기점을 낮추었다.
   ** Break even point = 손익분기점. Last resort: 최후의 수단. A final course action.

4. His debt has snowballed since last quarter.
   지난 분기부터 빚이 눈덩이처럼 불어났다.
   ** Increase rapidly in size, intensity.

5. His plan didn't materialize.
   그의 계획은 현실화되지 못했다.
   ** Appear in bodily form: become real.

6. The partner stabbed us in the back by selling company secrets to a rival company.
   동업자는 경쟁회사에게 회사비밀을 팔아 뒤통수를 쳤다(배반).
   ** To betray someone.

7. He built his entire business from scratch.
   그는 그 사업 전체를 처음부터 세웠다.
   ** From the beginning.

8. The drug is a cash cow for the company.
   그 약은 그 회사의 꾸준한 수입을 가져오는 품목이다.
   ** It will produce steady cash flow.

9. The stakes are too high to give it up.
   그것을 포기하기는 너무 가치(상업상)가 크다.
   ** A prize, reward.

10. It is a long shot that he can get the business.
    그가 그 사업을 (buyer로) 잡는 것은 승산이 희박하다.
    ** Only the slightest chance of success.

11. The firm will lower its overhead to increase its profit.
    그 회사는 이익을 올리려 경상비를 내릴 것이다.
    ** Fixed costs.

12. The US solar panel is at stake unless China restrains Its export.
    중국이 수출을 자제하지 않으면 미국 태양광 패널(생산)이 (경쟁에) 위험하다.
    ** At risk.

13. The steel co. had been the bread and butter for Gary area people in Indiana.
    그 철강회사는 게리-인디애나 주 지역 사람들에게 중요한 기본수입이었다.
    ** Considered basic forms of sustenance.

14. Wind energy will take off with president Obama's support.
    오바마의 지원으로 풍력(에너지 사업)은 뜰 것이다(상승).
    ** Become successful or popular.

15. Until the loan is approved, they can not spend working capital for durable goods.
    대출이 승인될 때까지는 시설비(장비, 기계 etc.)로 운영자금을 쓸 수 없다.
    ** 기계, 장비 같은 것.

16. The firm couldn't solidify its <u>dominant</u> position in the market.
    그 회사는 시장에 <u>지배적인</u> 위치를 굳힐 수 없었다.
    ** Most important, powerful, or influential. Solidify: to make solid.

17. Rental business of wedding dresses has ben establishing solid <u>niche market.</u>
    결혼 드레스를 임대하는 비즈니스는 견고한 틈새시장을 형성하고 있다.
    ** A specialized segment of the market for a particular kind of product or service:

Pick an incorrect word

A. GM future looks very _____ since Japanese car makers gained the vast car market share.
   ① bleak ② grave ③ grim ④ shallow

B. Some investors turn to _____ IT business again starting from the early 2000s.
   ① burgeoning ② lucrative ③ sprawling ④ stagnant

C. The steel industry might go _____ if the government did not help.
   ① south ② through the roof ③ under ④ up in smoke

** Answer: A-④, B-④, C-②

생활영어 기업 운영1-2

1. They had to grease the City-Hall's palm to get the government project.
   정부 공사를 받으려고 시청에게 뇌물을 주어야 했다.
   ** To bribe.

2. His business has been growing by leaps and bounds.
   그의 사업은 일취월장(급성장) 하고 있다.
   ** Grow or increase rapidly.

3. He bit off more than he can chew by opening another café.
   그는 너무 능력 이상으로 식당을 확장하였다.
   ** Try to do more than one is able to do.

4. The nuts and bolts of the movie industry are fashionable hype.
   영화 사업의 기본요소는 패션 있는 떠들석한 광고이다.
   ** 1. Nuts and bolts: the basic component.
      2. Hype: extravagant or intensive publicity or promotion.

5. The manager said his company can't afford to stay with the status quo.
   매니저는 현 상태에서 그대로 머물러만 있을 수는 없다고 말했다.
   ** The existing condition.

6. The company executives run a helter skelter to find investors.
   회사 간부들은 투자가들을 찾으러 허겁지겁 뛰어다닌다.
   ** Hurry and confusion. Turmoil.

7. He stretched his business too thin.
   그는 사업을 너무 벌려놓았다(확장).
   ** To try to do a lot of different things at the same time.

8. One employee blew the lid off the company's tax evasion.
   한 직원이 그 회사의 세금 탈세를 폭로하였다.
   ** To reveal the truth.

Pick the incorrect word

A. Japanese real estate investors have begun to _____ to invest again, but much more cautiously.

① count on   ② size up   ③ sound out   ④ test the water

B. When you apply for a mortgage loan, Pick _____ interest loan.

① adjustable   ② fixed   ③ floating   ④ soaring

*** Answer: A-①, B-④

Dun & Bradstreet Company

미국 회사로 미국에 있는 기업의 신용도나 기업상태를 평가하는 기업으로, 거래를 처음 시작하는 기업들의 신용도나 실적을 말해주는 기업이다. 첫번 거래할 회사의 신용도나 능력을 알려면 이 회사는 189불을 받고 한 기업의 정보를 제공한다. 새 기업을 시작할 때 중요한 정보이다.

The Dun & Bradstreet Holdings, Inc. is an American company that provides commercial data, analytics, and insights for businesses. Headquartered in Jacksonville, Florida, the company offers a wide range of
products and services for risk and financial analysis.

미국 기업의 대형 공모: GM, Standard Oil & Fire Stone

자동차회사(GM)와 정유회사(Standard Oil), 타이어회사(Firestone)들이 1945년부터 미국 내 25여 개 도시들의 전차(Tram, Electrical Street Car) 트랙을 제거하였다. 그들의 자동차, 정유, 타이어(Tire) 판매를 증가시키려 도시 교통인 전기차 철도(Rail)를 제거하였다. 많은 노선을 Gm 버스로 바꾸어서 현재 La 지역 고속도로 #5, #10, #405 교통 혼잡, 공해로 심각한 문제를 만들고 있다. 이 기업들은 미국 내에 이런 방법으로 기업을 확장하다가 고소를 당했다.

By 1945, Pacific Electric was inextricably in trouble, but the nail in their coffin actually had nothing to do with them. Company called National City Lines brought up the Los Angeles Railway only to rip up the tracks that sent their Yellow Cars—and by extension, Pacific Electric's Red Cars through the city streets to make way for a new fleet of buses, putting an end to the whole streetcar system in Los Angeles.

It just so happens that the principle investors in National City Lines were General Motors, Firestone Tire Company, and Standard Oil of California, and Phillips Petroleum. You know, a lot of folks who had a vested interest in the success of the automobile.

It didn't help that just four years later, those corporations were found guilty of "conspiring to acquire control of a number of transit companies, forming a transportation monopoly" and "conspiring to monopolize Sales of buses and supplies to companies owned by National City Lines" in violation of the 1890 Sherman Antitrust Act.

by History Daily- L.A. public transit system.

🔍 미국 대기업과 한국 가족재벌들의 비교

한국의 4대 기업들은 골목상권에 들어와 50,000개 이상 가맹점(Franchise)을 소유한 후 영세 상인들이 운영하는 편의점의 판매액이나 이익금의 35%를 본사가 받아간다. 미국의 본사와 한국 가족 재벌이 소유한 가맹점에서 받아가는 금액을 비교하면 왜 한국의 영세 상인들이 힘들게 살고 있는지 찾아볼 수 있다. 가맹점을 운영하는 한국의 영세 상인들은 본사에 35%를 내고, 미국 기업의 본사는 가맹점에서 4.5%에서 8%를 본사가 받아간다.

아래 한국 본사가 가져가는 이익금과 미국 본사가 가져가는 %.

	미국	한국
세븐일레븐	7~12	35
CU, YS25	35	?
MaCdonald	5	?
Burger King	4.5	?
KFC	4~5	?
Starbucks	7	?
Dunkin Donut	5.9	?
Subway	8	?
롯데 햄버거	?	?

Chapter 18-4.

금융 & 임금격차

Finance & Wage Gap

생활영어 금융1-1

1. The bank has a lien on his building.
   그 은행은 그의 건물을 담보로 잡고 있다.
   ** A right to keep possession of property belonging to another person.

2. The bank demands a bigger collateral for the loan.
   은행은 대출에 더 큰 담보물을 요구한다.
   ** An asset pledged by a borrower, to a lender (or a creditor) as security for a loan.

3. The bank laundered a few billions dollars of a Mexican drug firm.
   그 은행은 멕시코 마약 비즈니스의 수십억 불을 돈세탁하였다.
   ** An illegal act in which one makes illegally obtained money appears to be legally obtained.

4. His check is bounced because his checking account did not have enough money to cover.
   수표로 지급할 수표 계좌에 금액이 모자라 발행한 수표가 부도가 났다.
   ** A check that was used for payment, but it could not be processed because the check writer did not have sufficient Funds available to fund at the account.

5. Her CD matures at the end of next month.
   다음 달 말에 그 여성의 CD가 만기가 된다.
   ** CD (certificate of deposit) 정기예금.

6. Google bankrolled a solar energy project.
   G 회사는 태양열 에너지 프로젝트에 재정 지원하였다.
   ** Support financially.

7. He tried to capitalize on a bid with his dad's City Hall connection.
   아버지의 시청 빽으로 입찰에서 덕을 보려 했다.
   ** Take the chance to gain advantage from.

8. His friend blew his one month paycheck for a stock investment.
   그의 친구는 한 달 봉급을 증권투자에 다 날려버렸다.
   ** To move or be carried by or as if by wind or air.

9. P company stock has never fallen below the IPO price.
   P 회사 증권가격은 신규 상장 가격 이하로 하락한 적이 없다.
   ** Initial public offering.

10. In 1980s, heyday of CD rate was around 12%, then plunged to 0.9% in 2021.
    CD 전성기이던 1980s에는 이자가 12%였는데, 2021년에는 0.9%로 하락하였였다.
    ** The period of a person's or thing's greatest success.

11. Mr. Madoff had been keeping his customers in the dark about his embezzlement.
    M 씨는 고객(투자가)들에게 그의 착복을 감추고 있었다.
    ** To intentionally withhold information from someone.

12. The Federal Reserve Bank prime rate was 3.25%.
    연방은행이 꿔주는 고객(은행) 이자율은 3.25%였다.
    ** The current interest rate that financial institutions in the U.S. charges their best customers.

13. Don't bank on the buyer. They are negotiating with another firm.
    그 매입자를 기대하지 마십시오. 그들은 다른 공급자와 협상하고 있습니다.
    ** Count on, expect.

14. Pay off the loan shark the principal right away.
    당장 고리대금업자에게 원금을 갚으시오.
    ** A money lender who charges extremely high rates of interest.

15. Two brothers have been arguing over their dad's funeral expense which was nickel and dime.
    두 형제는 아버지의 약소한 장례식 경비로 싸우고 있다.
    ** Petty, not important.

16. What's pushing the Wall Street's rally?
   무엇이(이유) 증권가(WS) 증권가격을 급상승시키나?
   ** Sharp rise in stock price.

17. The accountant forgot to do reconciliation of the checking account.
   회계사는 수표 계좌 잔고를 은행계정 조정하는 일을 잊었다.
   ** 은행잔고 조정: 은행의 statement에서 발행한 수표의 돈을을 찾아가지 않은 (outstanding)돈이나 은행에 입금(intransit)을 반영시키는(refrect) 잔고 계산.

Pick an unfit word

A. He is _____ broke since the economy went down-turn.
   ① completely ② flat ③ stone ④ wholly

B. _____ speaks louder than truth in that society.
   ① Buck ② Dough ③ Long green ④ Marble

C. Federal Government had to _____ the failing GM to save the workers' job.
   ① bankroll ② finance ③ forfeit ④ subsidize

D. Cash _____ will affect the firm's future expansion.
   ① crunch ② distress ③ pinch ④ shortage

*** Answer: A-④, B-④, C-③, D-②

생활영어 금융1-2

1. His father decided to go for broke for the oil well.
   그의 아버지는 유전에 큰 모험을 걸었다.
   ** To risk everything in the hope of having great success.

2. He was born with a silver spoon in his mouth.
   그는 부잣집에서 태어났다.
   ** Born into a very wealthy family.

3. He lost his shirt from the investment of the gold mine.
   그집은 금광에 투자하여 전 재산을 날렸다.
   ** To lose everything.

4. Do you still believe in the car battery business? Then, Put your money where your mouth is.
   당신은 배터리 사업(이 장래가 있다고) 믿느냐?
   그렇다면 말만 하지 말고 그곳에 투자하시게.
   **You'll show with your actions that you mean what you say.
   ** To encourage people to do more than just talk about.

5. He is left holding the bag after the partner disappeared into thin air.
   그의 동업자가 어디로 사라지자(2) 빈손으로 남았다(1).
   ** (1) To be left empty-handed, Abandoned by others. (2) 사라지다.

6. He won't lend any money to the dead beat who used to be his buddy.
   그는 옛 친구였던 빚쟁이에게 돈을 빌려주지 않는다.
   ** Someone who owes money(빚을 갚지 않는 사람)

7. His stock prediction was right on the money.
   그의 증권 예측(주가 상승)은 옳았다.
   ** Completely right.

8. The CEO's demotion was a pocket book issue.
   그 회장의 강등은 돈(income) 문제였다.

** Billfold, purse, hand bag, income, money.

9. Hitting a jackpot comes <u>once in a blue moon.</u>
   횡재를 만난다는 것은 가뭄에 콩 나기이다.
   ** Very rarely.

10. He knows well <u>which side of the bread is buttered.</u>
    그는 어느 직위가 더 좋은지를 잘 알고 있다.
    ** The buttered side of a piece of bread has more value than the plain side, just like which position is better.

11. Toyota got a <u>wind-fall</u> from Obama's economic stimulus package.
    오바마 경제 촉진정책 덕분에 토요타 회사로 우연히 이익을 받았다.
    ** Unexpected gain or fortune. [바람에 떨어지는 사과같이]

12- A. He <u>cashed in on</u> his life insurance policy.
       그는 생명보험을 현금으로 받았다.
    B. The singer <u>cashed in on</u> his popularity.
       그 가수는 인기 덕분에 덕을 보았다.
    ** To obtain advantage or financial profit often used with.

Pick an incorrect word

A. His family is _____ sending his kids at Ivy League.
   ① affluent ② well-off ③ well rounded ④ well to do

B. When you apply for a mortgage loan, Pick _____ interest rate.
   ① adjustable ② fixed ③ floating ④ stagnant

C. The unknown buyer was willing to _____ $34 million for Monet's two paintings in London in 1998.
   ① cough up ② fork over ③ shell out ④ spill over

D. Investors are watching when the _____ price bottoms out.
① Dow Jones   ② FDIC   ③ NASDAQ   ④ S&P 500

*** Answer: A-③, B-④, C-④, D-②

임금 격차

지난 40년간 미국의 서민 생활은 살기 힘든 생활을 지속하여 왔는데 상위 10%의 국민들은 너무나 경제적으로 여유 있는 생활을 해왔다. 서민들을 지원하는 민주당에 책임을 넘기기는 이해가 안 되는 공화당의 경제 정책으로 최저 임금을 $7.20로 묶어왔다.

Economic Policy Institute

	1979년	2020년	Change
최저 10%	$ 31,000	$ 40,085	28%
평균 50%	$ 40,200	$ 59,000	48%
상위 10%	$ 102,000	$ 173,000	69%
최상 1%	$ 294,000	$ 823,000	179%

다시 말하면 미국 중류층 1년 월급은 자기 집 자식 한 명을 명문 사립대학에 보낼 1년 등록금 금액이다.

wage trends for the top 1.0% and other very high earners as well as for the bottom 90% during 2020. The upward distribution of wages from the bottom 90% to the top 1.0% that was evident over the period from 1979 to 2019 was especially strong in the 2020 pandemic year, yielding historically high wage levels and shares of all wages for the top 1.0% and 0.1%.

Correspondingly, the share of wages earned by the bottom 95% fell in 2020. This disparity in wage growth reflects a sharp long-term rise in the share of total wages earned by those at the very top: the top 1.0% earned 13.8% of all wages in 2020, up from 7.3% in 1979.

⟨ Economic Policy Institute ⟩

Chapter 18-5.

경 영

Management

백화점-Sears, 독점규제(Anti-Trust: Standard Oil & AT&T)

생활영어 경영1-1

1. Spencer pulled a string to aid Nancy Rgan's part in Hollywood.
   S는 N에게 할리웃 영화에 배역을 얻어 주려고 빽을 썼다.
   ** Make use of one's influence.

2. The union has been a thorn in the CEO's eyes (or side).
   노조는 그 회장의 눈엣가시였다.
   ** Persistent cause of annoyance.

3. Staffers are sick of their boss's nit Picking.
   직원들은 상사의 작은 트집에 질렸다.
   ** To be concerned with or find fault with insignificant details.

4. à his boss threw up his hands on the guy's constant tardiness.
   그 보스는 그 자의 끊임없는 지각에 두 손 들었다.
   **To express or indicate exasperated despair or hopelessness.

5. GE had a hard time filling his shoes after Jack retired.
   GE 회사는 Jack이 퇴직한 그의 지위를 채울 사람 찾는 데 힘이 들었다.
   ** To take someone's place or position.

6. Mike revealed the company's unfair promotion by sticking his neck out.
   M은 회사의 불공평한 진급(비리)에 대해 겁없이 밝혔다.
   ** Do or say something which other people are afraid to do.

7. Low-paying jobs have high turn-over rates.
   저임금 직장은 이직률이 높다.
   ** The percentage of employees that leave your Organization during a given time period.

8. His boss blamed his subordinate to save his neck.
   그의 보스는 자기(직위)를 지키려고 하급자를 비난하였다.
   ** To help someone avoid getting into trouble.

9. The newly employed worker needs more hands-on experience.
   그 신입사원은 실무경험이 더 필요하다.
   ** Relating to, being, or providing direct practical experience in the operation.

10. He took a leave of absence to tend her dying mom.
    그는 죽어가는 어머니를 돌보려고 휴직을 받았다.
    ** An employee is given permission to take time off from work for an extended period of time.

11. The average days of paid maternity leave given by companies are 8 weeks.
    회사가 월급을 지불해주는 임신 휴가는 평균 8주이다.
    ** A period of absence from work granted to a mother before after the birth of her child.

12. Amazon gave 10,000 workers a pink slip in 2022.
    아마존은 2022년에 만 명의 근로자에게 해고통지서를 보냈다.
    ** Notice of dismissal from employer.

13. FDA may bury hatchet with the anti-aging cream maker about its effectiveness.
    식약청은 젊어지는 크림 제조회사와 그 약 효과에 대한 싸움을 중단할지도 모른다.
    ** To make peace.

14. The CEO fell from grace when IRS revealed his cheating on the tax return.
    국세청이 그 회장이 세금 보고를 속인 사실을 밝히자 망신당했다.
    ** To lose respect.

15. The investment firm hires the cream of the crop to manage a budget of $ 8 billion.
    투자기업은 80억 불 재정관리 때문에 최고의 엘리트를 채용하였다.
    ** The very best of all.

16. His boss gets a few <u>perks</u> as he gets a company car and travel expense account.

   그의 보스는 회사 자동차와 여행 경비를 받는 특혜(보너스 등등)를 받는다.

   ** Extra bonus received in addition to regular wage.

17. Friction between management and union is an <u>inevitable</u> fact.

   경영진과 노조간의 마찰은 필연의 일이다.

   ** Unavoidable.
   ** Per Diem: sale calls 할 때 회사에서 하루에 주는 경비.

Pick the incorrect word

A. The president gave the _____ to make a new product.

   ① go ahead ② green light ③ nod ④ trial

B. His boss treats employees like (a) _____ .

   ① crumb ② dirt ③ door mat ④ trash

C. His _____ skill will put him to a key executive position.

   ① pragmatic ② prudent ③ savvy ④ vulnerable

D. His expansion plan had to be _____ due to the interest rate increase.

   ① expedited ② put it off ③ put on hold ④ shelved

E. The research department will _____ hundreds of thousands of dollars to develop a new product.

   ① infuse ② instill ③ pump ④ pour

F. His _____ skill will put him to a key executive position.

   ① deliberate ② pragmatic ③ prudent ④ savvy

   ** Answer: A-④, B-①, C-④, D-①, E-②, F-①

생활영어 경영1-2

1. The rank and file planned to organize union at Walmart.
   평사원들은 월마트 회사에서 노조를 만들 계획을 하였다.
   ** Average worker.

2. The manager raised the eyebrow when his subordinator threw away a bunch of documents on the floor.
   하급직원이 바닥에 서류를 집어던지자 매니저가 경악하였다.
   ** To show confusion, surprise, concern or disapproval, either literally.

3. His boss passed the buck to his predecessor to save his position.
   상관은 자기 직위를 보호하려고 전임자에게 책임을 전가하였다.
   ** To evade responsibility by passing it on to someone else.

4. Some people do not believe that a squeaky wheel gets the grease.
   요구를 많이 하는 사람이 요구로 보답을 먼저 받는다는 말을 어떤 사람은 믿지 않는다. [우는 아이 젖 먼저 준다와 유사한 의미]
   ** The person who complains the loudest about a problem receives help first.

5. The airline opened a can of worms when they negotiated pay increase of pilots. It triggered a new demand by a flight attendant Union.
   항공사가 조종사와 월급인상을 타협하자 스튜어디스 노조도 (덩달아) 새 임금인상 요구로 긁어 부스럼을 만들었다.
   ** Attempt to solve some problem, only to inadvertently complicate it and create even more trouble.
   ** 긁어 부스럼 만든다.

6. His boss has been breathing down his neck to fire him.
   그의 상사는 그를 퇴직시키려 주시하고 있다.
   ** Watching everything that they do.

7. The angry reporter has <u>blown the lid off</u> a company's price fixing.
   화가 난 기자는 그 회사의 가격조작을 <u>폭로하였다</u>.
   ** To reveal the truth.

8. The executive gets all the <u>fringe benefits</u> he can get, including company private jet.
   그 간부는 회사 비행기 같은, 회사의 모든 특혜를 받는다.
   ** Fringe benefit is a form of extra payment to employees.
   월급 이외에 회사에서 제공하는 <u>혜택(출장비, 보너스, 임신휴가)</u>

9. The owner <u>went through the mill</u> to build the factory.
   그 주인은 공장을 건설하려 <u>많은 고생을 하였다</u>.
   **Experience the suffering or discipline to bring one to a certain degree of knowledge or skill.

10. Degree <u>per se</u> does not guarantee success; often, luck is also necessary.
    학위 <u>한 가지로만</u> 성공을 보장받지 못한다. 자주 행운도 필요하다.
    ** By itself.

11. He shouldn't be a governor as he has too many <u>axes to grind</u>.
    그는 너무 <u>개인 이익을 추구하여</u> 주지사가 되어서는 안 되었다.
    ** A selfish aim or motive [사리사욕이 많은]

12. GE said they should adopt <u>two tier system</u> to compete with Chinese products.
    GE 회사는 중국산 제품과 경쟁하려면 두 가지 임금제도를 적용해야 한다고 말했다.
    ** A type of payroll system in which one group of workers receives lower wages and/or employee benefits than another.

13. The management will adjust old <u>per diem</u> for sales call according to rising inflation.
    경영진은 상승하는 물가고에 따라 고객 방문 시 드는 <u>하루 경비</u>를 조절할 것이다. [sales calls 때 쓰는 하루 경비]
    ** Daily allowances paid to employees to cover costs it occurs while on a business trip.

14. He finally came to terms with his demotion.
    그는 결국 그의 강등을(낮은 지위에 대한 현실을) 받아들였다.
    ** To accept the fact(get it over it, 분노, 수치| etc.)

Pick the incorrect word

A. Mexico government's _____ has been dragging its economy poor nation.
   ① cronyism ② euphemism ③ favoritism ④ nepotism

B. The executive is _____ after a newspaper reveale.
   ① in hot water ② on the hot seat ③ under fire ④ under a storm

*** Answer: A-②, B-④

생활영어 경영1-3

1. All workers rolled up their sleeves.
   직원 모두 소매를 걷어 부쳤다. [열심히 일하려]

2. They blame their boss behind his back.
   그들은 등 뒤에서 상관을 비난한다.

3. He is in charge on weekends.
   주말에는 그가 책임자이다.

4-1. He stands up to his boss's abuse.
   그는 보스의 괴롭힘에 대항하여 일어났다.

4-2. He stands up for his peer's right.
   그는 동료의 권리를 위해 일어난다. [반기, 반항]

🔍 백화점(Sears) & 독점규제: Standard Oil & AT&T

1892년에 기업을 시작하여 3,500개의 백화점으로 성장한 Sears 회사는 1973년에는 시카고에 110층 건물에 본사를 세웠던 기업이 2018년 파산 선고를 하였다. 신용카드(Discover) 금융과 자동차 부품사업을 크게 벌린 기업은 컴퓨터로 주문받고 배달해주는 아마존 회사와 월마트(WalMart) 기업에 밀려 파산하였다.

Investopedia

Who Killed Sears? Fifty Years on the Road to Ruin. Sears Holdings (SHLD) filed for Chapter 11 bankruptcy on Oct.15, 2018. A wave of store closures and deals in desperate attempts to stay afloat failed to save the struggling retailer,that listed $6.9 billion in assets and $11.3 billion in liabilities….

Forbes

WEB Oct 15, 2018 · Make no mistake about it: Eddie Lampert's financial deconstruction of Sears Holdings is the No. 1 reason the retailer is now in bankruptcy, having filed for Chapter 11 bankruptcy today….
Yes, Blame Eddie Lampert For Sears' Bankruptcy, But Don't

반독점(Anti-trust) Sherman Act

스탠다드 오일(Standard Oil), AT & T.

1984년 미국정부는 전화회사가 지방전화 통화운영과 모든 장비를 독점하여 7개 지역으로 분리시켜 7개 독립회사가 되었고, 이 독점적인 파워를 가졌던 AT&T가 분리되자 T-mobile, Verizon 회사가 나타나 소비자들이 선택할 수 있는 회사가 증가하였다.

Historically, AT&T controlled a large potion of the phone market through its "Bell System," essentially act monopoly by owning most local telephone operating companies and dominating the long-distance service, allowing them to exert significant control over both phone equipment and service provision; however, due to antitrust concerns, the company was forced to break up in 1982, creating several smaller regional companies known as "Baby Bells," significantly reducing their overall market dominance.

정유회사 스탠다드 오일은 처음으로 Billionaire 부자가 되었다. 1870에 설립하여 1911년까지 기업활동을 하다가 정부의 독점기업으로 Anti-Trust법에 검거되어 대법원 판결로 문을 닫고, 정부는 34개의 회사로 분리시켰다.

The oil co. had eliminated most competition within Ohio that was 1/3 of total US production in 1873. By 1878, Standard oil controlled 90% of all oil refined in the US. It emplyed a variey cut-throat strategies and tactics to undermine its competitors. By University of Calf. Berkeley.

생활영어 경제, 마케팅 - 협상1-1

1. Our staff have been waiting for them <u>to lay the Cards on the table.</u>
   우리 직원들은 협상의 조건을 그들이 밝히기를 기다리고 있다.
   **Reveal one's or intentions.

2. We failed to read between the lines during the negotiation.
   우리들은 협상 도중에 그들의 숨은 뜻을 찾는 데 실패하였다.
   ** To try to understand someone's real intentions.

3. China has a <u>cutting edge</u> on labor cost over European products.
   중국은 인건비에서 유럽 제품보다 장점을 가지고 있다.
   ** Something an advantage over others.

4. They are <u>back pedaling</u> before the ink dries up.
   (계약서에) 잉크가 마르기 전에 그들은 계약을 취소하려 한다.
   ** To withdraw.

5. The seller was in panic when <u>the chips are down.</u>
   사정이 힘들어지자 판매자는 공포에 처했다.
   ** All the bets are in a serious or difficult situation.
   ** panic: sudden sense of fear.

6. It will be a <u>train wreck</u> to us If the firm pulls out of the negotiation.
   그들이 협상을 중단한다면 우리에게는 대참사가 될 것이다.
   ** A disastrous situation.

7. We suggested a long lunch to the supplier to <u>buy time.</u>
   시간을 벌려고 우리는 긴 점심을 가지자고 판매원에게 제안했다.
   ** To delay an imminent action or decision.

8. Let's get down to the <u>nitty gritty</u> of the maintenance costs.
   운영경비의 자세한 사항에 대한 토론에 들어 갑시다.
   ** The essential substance or details of a matter.

9. Both sides are dragging their feet for weeks over price.
   양측은 가격 때문에 몇 주간 (계약)지연을 시키고 있다.
   ** Delay.

10. The explanation of additional charges just doesn't add up.
    더 첨가된 청구액의 설명은 이해가 안 간다.
    ** Do not make sense.

11. If you give them an inch they'll take a mile.
    한 치의 양보를 해주면 그들은 무척 많은 양보를 요구할 것이다.

12. Sales man speaks a mile a minute to confuse the customer.
    판매사원은 손님을 혼동하게 하려 말을 빨리한다.

13. The supplier will give us great advice—which comes with strings attached.
    그 공급자는 우리에게 좋은 충고를 해줄 것이다. 그렇지만 조건이 붙어있다. [많은 서비스 charger가 있다.]

14. The high maintenance fee for the treadmills is a sticking point If you rent them.
    러닝머신을 임대한다면 높은 유지비가 걸림돌이다.
    ** Something preventing progress.

15. Buying our product by P company is still up in the air.
    P 회사의 우리 회사 상품 매입은 아직도 미정이다.
    ** Not settled, uncertain.

16. The clock is ticking. We should fish the project at the end of next week.
    시간이 다해 갑니다(서두릅시다). 다음 주말까지는 그 프로젝트를 끝내야 합니다.
    ** Warning that there is not much time.

17. They are at the stage of finishing touches.
    그들은 (계약을) 마무리 짓는 단계입니다.
    ** A final adjustment of something.

18. The garment factory reached a <u>tentative agreement</u> with them to receive fabric that is running out in a month.

봉제 공장은 한 달 내에 천이 떨어져서 (급해서) 잠정적인 합의를 보았다.

** Temporary agreement.

19. Let's <u>wrap it up</u> before the end of this year.

연말 전에 일을 마무리 지읍시다.

** Close, close out, complete.

20. They think he <u>put two and two together</u> and realized that his partner had been stealing from him.

그가 증거로 추정해 보면 그의 동업자가 훔친 것이라고 그들은 생각한다.

** To draw a conclusion based upon the given evidence.

✎ 주의해 둘 표현(expression)

A. I am <u>afraid</u> we can take the offer.

우리가 그의 제안을 나는 받아들일수 없다.

**afraid에 부정의 뜻이 들어있다.

B. we <u>couldn't agree more</u> on the delay.

우리는 그 지연(작전)에 (양측이) 동의한다.

Pick an incorrect word

A. The market is _____ with cheap TV sets.

① clogged ② flooded ③ inundated ④ saturated

B. They are about to _____ a deal after a few months negotiation.

① cut ② reach ③ strike ④ tie

** Answer: A-①, B-④

생활영어 경제, 마케팅 - 협상1-2

1. They have been playing hard ball to cut the price.
   그들은 가격을 깎으려 강수를 두고 있다.
   ** They use every legitimate resource and strategy available to them to gain an advantage over.

2. He has no problem to compete with any big firm if he competes from a level playing field.
   공정한 조건이 주어진다면 그는 어느 대기업과 경쟁을 해도 문제가 없다.
   ** Fair competition.

3. The supplier turned the table on us by bringing up our late reply.
   우리의 늦은 답변을 트집잡아 판매자가 유리한 입장으로 전세가 바뀌었다.
   ** To gain the advantage by reversing the situation.

4. We don't have all day, please, cut to the chase.
   시간이 많지 않으니 제발 요점을 말해주시오.
   ** Get to the point.

5. They threw a curve ball whenever they were cornered for his excuse.
   핑계를 말하다가 그들이 구석에 몰리면 혼란한 말로 우리를 혼동하게 만들었다.
   ** To do something deceptive or confusing.

6. His sincere offer couldn't cut the ice with the buyers.
   그의 진심인 제안은 구매자에게 만족을 주지 못했다.
   ** To be very impressive, influential, or satisfactory to a person.
   ** To do something deceptive or confusing

7. M. company kept its second offer up it's sleeve.
   M회사는 협상에서 두 번째 제안할 비밀을 숨겨 놓았다.
   ** To have secret plans.

8. GE's appliance has been a <u>household name</u> in the USA.
   GE 전자제품은 미국에서 가정용 브랜드로 잘 알려져 있다.
   ** A thing that is well known by the public.

9. His second offer looks <u>bona fide</u>.
   그의 두 번째 제안은 진실성이 있는 것 같다.
   ** Genuine.

10. The firm has been <u>beating around the bush</u> about why the shipping had been delayed.
    왜 운송이 늦어지는지 말은 하지 않고 딴소리만 하고 있다.
    ** To avoid getting to the point of an issue.

11. His investment in the Nickel mine <u>hit the bull's eye</u>.
    그의 니켈 광산에 대한 투자는 (이익을 내는 데) 명중하였다.
    ** They are exactly right about something or achieve the best result possible.

12. The defense contractor kept the new missile <u>under wraps</u>.
    방위산업 기업은 새 미사일을 숨겨두었다.
    ** Keeping it a secret.

13. The sleazy contractor still <u>wheels and deals</u> to win the lucrative City contract.
    간교한 건설업자는 시청의 이익 많은 공사를 받으려고 수단방법을 가리지 않는다.
    ** They use a lot of different methods to achieve what they want in business or politics. The art of hustling.

14. The firm will lower the selling price as a <u>last ditch effort</u> to survive.
    그 회사는 생존하려고 최후의 수단으로 판매가격을 낮추려고 하였다.
    ** Last attempt.

Pick an unfit word

A. They have to work hart to survive at _____ competition.
   ① cut throat ② dog eat dog ③ swift ④ vicious

B. Marketing staff _____ huge size of TV sets.
   ① flirt with ② kick around ③ shuffle with ④ toy with

C. They compete _____ with the huge firm to keep its territory.
   ① eyeball to eyeball ② fist to fist ③ head to head ④ toe to toe

D. China already started to _____ out electric cars.
   ① churn ② crank ③ mend ④ roll

*** Answer: A-③, B-③, C-②, D-③

🔍 마케팅(marketing- Amazon Co. 〈Michigan University〉.

자기 집 차고에서 30년 전 책을 팔기 시작하여 Jeff는 현재 45개 국가와 미국 50개 주에 2022년에 5천백삼식억 달러를 판매하였고, 판매 품목은 6억 아이템이다. 신발부터 컴퓨터, 음식물부터 아이들 장난감까지, 60%의 중소기업 품목을 팔아주며 기업이 성장하였다.

More than 60% of sales in the Amazon store come from Independent sellers - most of which are small and medium-sized businesses. In 2023, US-based sellers sold more than 4.5 billion items—an average of 8,600 items every minute.

New York Times

WEB Aug 20, 2021 · And according to their estimates, people spent More than $610 billion on Amazon over the 12 months ending in June. Walmart on Tuesday posted sales of $566 billion for the 12 months ending in July.

How Amazon Managed to Dethrone Walmart – The New York Times

Havard Business Review

WEB November 17, 2020. Sunil Gupta, Harvard Business School professor, has spent years studying successful digital strategies, companieand leaders, and he's made Amazon and its legendary CEO Jeff ...

> How Jeff Bezos Built One of the World's Most Valuable

🔍 마케팅 전략- Amazon

In 2023, there were over 600 million products listed on Amazon; 12 million or 2% of these were through Amazon's own brands and 98% were through third-party vendors. Amazon is the 5 th largest company on the planet, with a market cap of $1.7 billion generating a net income of $26.3 billion in 2021.

Amazon's marketing strategy is truly global, making the company an international brand name. Not only is Amazon well-known, they're the source for e-commerce purchases with an estimated 65% of US citizens used ···

Unpacking Amazon's World-Dominating Marketing Strategy\ | Marketing Strategy

Chapter 19.

직장 & 노조

Workplace & Labor Union

생활영어 직장

1. Low income family had a hard time providing a <u>roof over their head</u> during the Covid 19.
   저임금 가족들은 코로나 전염병 시기에 주거지 구하기조차 힘들었다.
   ** Basic shelter.

2. <u>Sweat shop</u>: Tyson employees wear adult diapers because they are not allowed proper breaks in 2016.
   노예처럼 부려먹는 직장: 타이슨 직원들은 적절히 쉬는 시간을 허락받지 못해 (근무시간에) 성인 기저귀를 차야 했다.
   ** Workplace employing workers at low wages, for long hours, and under poor conditions.

3. She quitted the hospital job because of the long <u>grave yard shift</u>.
   긴 밤 근무 때문에 그 여성은 병원 직장을 그만두었다.
   ** Night shift(11pm~7am)

4. His mom has been <u>wearing the pants</u> after her husband died.
   그의 아버지가 사망하고, 그의 어머니가 가정을 꾸려가는 가장이 되었다.
   ** To be the person in a relationship who is in control.

5. The rest of workers had to <u>bite the bullet</u> since the factory cut down 30% of the workforce.
   공장이 인력을 30% 감소시키자 직원들은 힘들게 버텨야 했다.
   ** To brace oneself against pain or a difficult experience.

6. His supervisor, <u>a jack of all trades</u>, has been a back-bone of the factory.
   그의 보스는 그 공장의 기둥이 된 능숙한 기술자이다.
   ** A person who has many different work skills. 맥가이버?

7. Big firms still have a <u>glass ceiling</u> on females in Asia.
   동양의 대기업들은 아직도 여성들에게 눈에 안 보이는 제약을 하고 있다.
   ** A barrier that prevents specific individuals from advancing to leadership roles in organizations.

8. Insubordination is critical problem since their boss fell ill.
   보스가 아픈 이후 직원들의 불복종은 심각한 문제이다.
   ** Defiance of authority.

9. We have been close peers through thick and thin for 20 years.
   우리는 20년간 희로애락을 같이한 동료이다.
   ** No matter how difficult it is.

10. He twiddles his thumbs whenever his boss steps out of his office.
    상사가 사무실만 비우면 하릴없이 빈둥거린다.
    ** Do nothing while you are waiting for something to happen.

11. The labor union was outraged when the politician turned his back.
    그 정치가가 등을 돌리자 노조는 분노하였다.
    ** To change one's position later.

🖉 노조에 관계된 단어

1. sweet-heart contract
   기업과 노조 간부 간의 (불법)계약
2. close shop
   노조원만 고용하는 직장
3. wild cat strike
   노조협회에서 허락받지 않은 파업
4. scab
   노조원이 파업하는 동안 다른 사람들이 일하는 직원(피딱지)
5. yellow dog contract
   노조에 가입하지 않겠다는 직원과 회사 간의 계약

Pick an incorrect word

A. Berkeley professor Reich said it is _____ situation because S&P 500's CEO income went up 299 times while minimum wages increased just 3 times in the last 60 years in the USA.

① bleak ② grave ③ grim ④ uncertain

B. His family has a hard time to _____ with the minimum wage, that is $ 7.25 per hour in Pennsylvania.

① get by ② float ③ make ends meet ④ scrape by

C. Poverty pushes 122 million of children to risky job with ____ pay in south Asia.

① harsh ② meager ③ measly ④ paltry

*** Answer: A-④, B-②, C-①

생활영어 마케팅

1. Manager has been <u>beating around bush</u> why the store didn't refund the returned goods.
   상품을 돌려보냈는데 돈을 보내주지 않고 매니저가 딴소리만 하고 있다.
   **To avoid getting to the point of an issue.

2. The demotion was a <u>kick in the teeth</u> to her after she returned from maternity leave.
   임신 휴가 후에 돌아오자 낮은 직위로 보낸 것은 <u>너무한 짓</u>이다.
   ** Treat people badly.

3. The boss <u>took for granted</u> when all employees worked so hard to finish the project on time.
   제시간에 과제를 마치려 전 직원들이 열심히 일했을 때 보스는 <u>고마워하지 않고 그러려니</u> 해버렸다.
   ** Fail to properly appreciate.

4. Garment workers are <u>fed up with</u> the paycheck according to piece work.
   봉제공장 직원들은 만든 작업량에 따른 봉급 지불에 <u>질렸다</u>.
   ** Tired. piece-work: 만든 수량에 따라 봉급을 주는 제도.

5. Engineers have been <u>leaning over backwards</u> to solve the missile's defect.
   엔지니어들은 미사일의 결점을 해결하려 <u>열심히 노력하였다</u>.
   ** To try very hard. To expend a lot of energy or effort to do something.

6. He couldn't be promoted because He didn't <u>cut the mustard.</u>
   그는 <u>임무를 다하여</u> 일하지 않아 진급을 할 수 없었다.
   ** Surpass the desired standard or performance. Reach the required standard.

7. He attends evening class to fall back on if current company closes down.
   현재 직장이 문을 닫을 가능성을 생각해 차선책으로 (다른 직장을 찾을 생각에) 학교를 다닌다.
   ** To begin to use someone or something held in reserve.

8. His boss pulls rank on us to do his hard work.
   그의 상급자는 힘든 일을 우리에게 시키려 높은 지위를 이용한다.
   ** To use one's superior rank to gain an advantage over.

9. Female workers didn't get a fair shake when they faced a pay cut.
   여성직원들은 봉급 감봉 때 공정한 대우를 받지 못했다.
   ** Fair deal.

10. If you don't pull your weight, the company will let you go.
    당신이 당신의 임무를 다하지 않으면 회사가 당신을 해고시킬 것이다.
    ** Do one's fair share of work.

11. "Capitalism is off the rails." Professor Reich said. CEOs make 320 times more than average workers in 2020.
    자본주의는 통제할 수 없다고 Reich 교수가 말하였다.
    2020년 기업회장은 평사원보다 320배의 월급을 받는다고 말하였다.
    ** Someone or something that is uncontrollable.

Pick an unfit word

A. Some of the workers _____ their boss to get a fat paycheck.
   ① brown nose ② butter up ③ kiss ass ④ lend a hand to

B. He used to work _____ to get a promotion.
   ① butt off ② finger to the bone ③ slack off ④ tail off

C. 11 million people are living in _____ area in Brazil.
   ① gorge ② shanty town ③ skid row ④ slum

D. Hundreds of thousands worker are in fear of _____ from employers when they try to organize unions.
   ① debate ② intimidation ③ retaliation ④ threat

*** Answer: A-④, B-③, C-①, D-①

🔍 à Slave Labor

미국 남부 닭처리 공장(packaging)에서 일하는 직원들은 화장실 가는 시간과 휴식시간(coffee break)이 맞지 않아 성인 기저기를 차고 일해왔다.
*** 2024년에도 이런 미국 기업들이 있다. ***

In many large scale chicken factories, workers are routinely denied bathroom breaks -- leading some to urinate or defecate on the line, or even wear diapers to work, according to a Thursday report from human rights organization, Oxfam. Senator Berni Sanders: "The $7.25 an hour federal minimum wage is a starvation wage. It must be raised to a living wage – at least $17 an hour," said Sanders. "In the year 2023 a job should lift you out of poverty, not keep you in it. At a time of massive income and wealth inequality and record-breaking corporate profits.

Estimated to benefit nearly 28 million workers, or 19 percent of the working population, the Raise the Wage Act of 2023 would raise the federal minimum wage to $17 per hour over five years

WASHINGTON, July 25 – Sen. Bernie Sanders (I-Vt.), July 25, 2023
NEWS: Sanders, Scott, 29 DemocraticSenators,IntroduceLegislation to Raise the Minimum Wage to $17 by 2028, Benefitting Nearly 28 Million Workers Across America ≫ Senator Bernie Sanders (senate.gov).

Harvest Public Media investigation found that the more than 500,000 men and women who work in slaughterhouses and meat-processing plants have some of the most dangerous factory jobs in America. Government fines for abuses are low and lines speeds are so fast that workers are often crippled for life with repetitive motion, the investigation found. In a report issied last year called " No Relief," Oxfam charged that workers at the four largest U.S. poultry companies.

〈4-26-2017 / NPR〉

🔍 아직도 미국에서 최저임금 $7.25을 받는 주(state)

남부: Alabama, Georgia, Kentucky, Mississippi.
Texas, Tennessee, South Carolina, Louisiana.
중부: Indiana, Iowa, Kansas, Oklahoma.
북부: Utah, Wisconsin, Wyoming.
Pennsylvania, New Hampshire.

연방정부의 최저임금보다 주에서 최저임금을 올린 주

〈동부〉 Washington D.C.: $17.00, New Jersey: $15.13.
New York: $15.00, Massachusetts: $15.00.
Connecticut: $15.69, Maryland: $15.00.
Rhode Island: $14.

〈서부〉 California: $16. Oregon: $14, Washington: $16.28
Hawaii: $14. Colorado: $14. Arizona: $14.35.
Illinois:$14

Minimum Wage Rates by State 2024 (minimum-wage.org)

Chapter 20-1.

정치 - 정부

Politics - Government

🔍 국가별 부패 Index(Corruption Perception Index) in 2023

Denmark: 90   Finland: 87
Singapore: 83   Germany: 78
Japan: 73   France: 71
England: 71   USA: 69
S. Korea: 63   Italy: 51

2023 Corruption Perceptions Index: Explore the – Transparency.org

생활영어 정치1-1

1. Assad of Syria has been <u>cracking down on</u> his own people who have been protesting against his dictatorship for 10 some years.
   시리아의 독재자 Assad는 10여 년간 독재에 항거하는 시민들을 <u>탄압하고 있었다</u>.
   ** Suppress.

2. Assad, Syrian dictator, <u>beefed up</u> military power with Russian support, killing more than 300,000 his own people.
   시리아의 독재자 아사드는 러시아의 지원을 받아 권력을 <u>강화시키며</u> 300,000명 이상의 자기 국민들을 살해하였다.
   ** To make something stronger.

3. Ukraine people are <u>up in arms</u> against Russia's invasion since early.
   2022 우크라이나 사람들은 2022년 러시아 침공에 <u>봉기</u>를 들었다.
   ** Protesting vigorously about something.

4. Some people believe the Fed keeps UFO facts <u>in the dark</u>.
   어떤 사람들은 (미국) 정부기관이 UFO 사실을 <u>숨기고</u> 있다고 믿는다.
   ** To keep someone uninformed. The Fed =연방정부기관.

5. The senator requested a TV interview to set the record straight.
   그 상원의원은 정확한 사실을 밝히려 TV 인터뷰를 요청하였다.
   ** To provide the facts about something that people have false understanding or idea.

6. The dictator has been doing musical chairs with his cronies whenever citizens are furious at his policy.
   독재자는 그의 정책에 시민들이 분노하면 같은 추종자들을 돌려가며 인사이동을 해왔다.
   ** Any situation involving a number of people in a series of Interrelated Changes.

7. The FDA decided to foot the bill for Covid-19.
   식약청은 코로나 바이러스 백신 경비를 국민을 위해 국가가 대신 지급하기로 결정하였다.
   ** Pay for something.

8. Cliton's sex scandal with an intern was a black eye in the White House.
   백악관에서 클린턴의 인턴과의 섹스 스캔들은 망신이었다.
   ** Dishonor or disgrace.

9. The state government subsidy for college tuition has been a drop in the bucket.
   주 정부의 대학교 학비 지원금은 너무 미흡하였다.
   ** Very small.

10. None of us really understand his decision. There is no rhyme or reason.
    아무도 그의 결정이 우리에게는 이해가 안 간다(논리적이 아닌).
    ** No logical reason.

11. Ukraine women made Molotov cocktails to defend their country against Russia.
    우크라이나 여성들은 러시아에 대항하여 국가를 방어하려 화염병을 만들었다.
    ** A glass bottle containing a flammable substance such as gasoline, alcohol.

12. Myanmar(Burmar) military government clamped down viciously on the protesting citizens.
    미얀마(버마) 군사정부는 항거하는 시민들을 악랄하게 압박하였다.
    ** Suppress.

13. Uyghur people have been at odds with Chinese Government since 1955.
    위구르 국민들은 중국정부와 1955부터 갈등이 있어왔다.
    ** In conflict.

14. Mr. Trump orchestrated a political Coup d'état to be a president again by claiming the 2020 election was fixed(rigged) in 2021.
    트럼프는 2020 선거가 조작되었다고 주장하며 다시 대통령이 되려고 쿠테타(전복)를 조직하였다.
    ** Violent overthrow.

15. Angry father took the law in his own hands when his son was beaten up by a neighborhood guy.
    아들이 동네 남자에게 폭행당하자 그 아버지는 (경찰을 통하지 않고) 직접 보복하였다.
    ** 법의 절차를 밟지 않고 자신이 직접 보복하다.

16. The City added another ordinance to reduce fire accidents. But Landlords claim it is another bureaucratic red tape to add Additional fire alarm system.
    시청은 화재를 줄인다고 새 규정을 첨가하였다. 그러나 집주인(건물주)들은 관료들의 거추장스러운 규정을 더 첨가한 것이라고 주장한다.
    ** Hinders or prevents action by big systems.

17. The Ruling party dangles the carrot to the minority party to pass their lucrative bill for them.
    여당은 이권이 많은 법안을 통과시키려 야당에게 당근(reward)을 흔들어 댄다.
    ** To try to entice one with the promise of a reward.
    carrot and stick(상벌)에서 나온 변형

18. The Right wing congressmen became a mere rubber stamp when the Korean military dictator became the president in Korea for a few decades.
   한국의 군부 독재자가 대통령이 되자 우익 국회의원들은 십여 년간 단지 거수기였다.
   ** Approve automatically without proper consideration.

19. Congress allocates nearly 5,000 earmarks totaling $9 billion In 2022.
   국회는 2022년 5천 개 배정받은 프로젝트로 90억 불을 배정하였다.
   ** Fund that sets aside for a specific purpose.
   [꼭 필요하지 않은 프로젝트에도 선거자금 지원한 기업들에게 보답하느라 일거리를 만들어주는 때 자주 쓰임.]

20. Abortion issue has been a hot potato in the USA.
   낙태수술 이슈는 미국에서 다루기 힘든 문제(골치거리)였다.
   ** A controversial issue.

21. The CEO doubled down on his investment and hit it big.
   회장은 투자를 증가시켜 크게 성공하였다.
   ** To significantly increase or strengthen effort.

Pick an unfit word

A. During the Iraq war, Kurdish citizens became a target. It turned into _____ that killed nearly 182,000 Kurdish people.
   ① genocide ② massacre ③ revenge ④ wholesale slaughter

B. A newspaper said Bush gave Israel the _____ to invade Palestine in Dec. 2008.
   ① green light ② nod ③ permission ④ revoke

*** Answer: A-③, B-④

생활영어 정치1-2

1. <u>Good riddance!</u> The dictator Saddam of Iraq was arrested by a secret American army unit.

   천만다행이다. 미군의 비밀 군인 조직이 이라크의 독제자 사담을 납치하였다.

   ** To express relief at being free of a troublesome or unwanted person.

2. Entire world <u>raised eyebrows</u> when Putin invaded Ukraine.

   푸틴이 우크라이나를 침략하자 전세계가 <u>충격이었다.</u>

   ** To elicit shock.

3. The Germans decided to <u>pull the plug on</u> the nuclear power project.

   독일은 핵발전소 지원을 <u>중단</u>하기로 결정했다.

   ** To discontinue.

4. NATO leaders ran <u>helter skelter</u> when Russia invaded Ukraine in 2022.

   나토의 지도자들은 2022년 러시아가 <u>우크라이나를 침략하자</u> 허둥지둥하였다.

   ** In disorderly haste or confusion. chaos and disorder.

5. The Congress should pass the law to reduce the pollution problem, but they have been <u>kicking the can down the road.</u>

   국회는 공해를 줄이는 법을 통과시켜야 하는데 <u>지연만 시키고 있다.</u>

   ** To put off work on an issue for a later time.

6. Haiti has been a complete <u>basket case</u> even though UN tried to <u>lend a hand</u> to the nation.

   하이티는 UN이 도우려 해도 <u>구제불능</u>의 국가로 머물러 있다.

   ** A country or organization that is in severe financial or economic difficulty. Lend a hand: help.

7. They have not <u>come to grips</u> with what happened to China and Korea World War II.

   제2차 대전 때 UN은 중국과 한국에 무엇이 발생했는지 그 문제를 잘 파악하여 처리하지 못했다.

** To deal with something skillfully or efficiently.

8. The world had been taken aback when the military group arrested president Aung San Suu Kyi in Myanmar.
미얀마의 군부조직은 대통령 아웅산 수치를 체포하자 세계는 놀랐다.
* To startle or shock.

9. Ukraine asked NATO for more tanks and missiles to arm to the teeth against Russia.
우크라이나는 러시아에 대항해 방위력을 강화시키려고 나토에 탱크와 미사일을 더 많이 요청하였다.
** Heavily armed with critical weapons.

10. The US. Red Cross is in a Catch 22 situation when it comes to the economic sanctions due to the poor North Koreans.
미국 적십자는 미국의 북한에 대한 경제제재로 인해 가난한 북한 국민 때문에 딜레마에 처해있다.
** Dilemma. novel name of Mr. Heller.

11. Poor village people thumbed their's noses at the city of Rio de Janeiro when the city asked to clean the village for the Olympics.
리우 올림픽 때 시청 직원들이 가난한 지역 주민들에게 청소를 하라고 요청하자 웃기지 마(요청을 무시해)라고 반응했다.
** To express contempt or a lack of respect. 반항적으로 엿먹으라는?

12. The politician is hunkering down until people's anger dies down after he broke his campaign promise.
그 정치가가 선거 때 약속을 어기고 시민들의 분노가 사라질 때까지 몸을 낮추고 있다. [숨어있는 상태]
** To squat down near the floor. prepare oneself for hard work to find a shelter.

13. Mr. Biden, president of the USA, ups the ante by calling Putin a dictator.
미국 대통령 바이든은 푸틴 대통령을 독재자라고 불러 모험을 높였다(cold war).
** Increase what is at stake or under discussion. [무역전쟁, cold war를 일으킬 가능성]

Pick an unfit word

A. Under the leadership of Pol Pot, Cambodia's prime minister, From 1975 till 1979. he committed _____ , estimated 1.7 to 2.2 million. It has been known as "the Killing Fields."

① dismantle ② genocide ③ massacre ④ wholesale slaughter

B. The government is conducting business behind closed doors, keeping it under the _____ .

① hat ② desk ③ rug ④ wraps

***Answer: A-①, B-②

🔍 부패해지는 국가들

The global trend of weakening justice systems is reducing accountability for public officials, which allows corruption to thrive.

전 세계 관료와 정치가들의 부패가 증가하여 미국은 70점 미만으로 하락하여 69점이 되었다.

- The Fed: 연방정부기관, Capital Hill: 국회, DOJ : 법무부, Pentagon: 국방부, FDA: 식약청, S.S. number: 한국의 주민등록번호 같은 번호.

인도의 부패와 빈부 차이

인도가 영국의 식민지에서 해방되고 민주주의가 된 지 80년이 되어가도 일용직(비정규직) 여성, 막노동자들은 하루에 $ 4.60을 받는데, 대재벌은 167명이 되었다. 그 재벌들의 재산이 총 $773 billion이고, 인도의 비정규직이 80%이며, 13억 인구가 하루에 $3.10로 살아간다고 CNN이 보도하였다. 제일 하층인 다릿(Dalit)은 1천 600만 명인데, 이 계급의 학생들은 교실 제일 뒤에 앉아서 공부하며 다른 학생과 같은 우물을 쓰지 않는다.

India's Inequality— IMF

Our analysis has important implications for the understanding of the unequal representation of status groups as it sheds light on an important, yet so far unexplored, aspect of the political process. Since the misrepresentation of political agendas occurs at the very beginning of the policy-making process, the consequences are potentially even…

Caste System by Human Right Org

Despite its constitutional abolition in 1950, the practice of untouchability the imposition of social disabilities on persons by reason of birth into a particular caste remains very much a part of rural India.

Representing over one- sixth of Indiaís population or some 160 million people Dalits endure near complete social ostracization. Untouchables may not cross the line dividing their part of the village from that occupied by higher castes. They may not use the same wells, visit the same temples, or drink from the same cups in tea stalls. Dalit children are frequently made to sit at the back of classrooms.

12/23/2022/ NPR

Chapter 20-2.

정치 - 입법부

Politics – Legislature

🔍 U.S. Presidential Election in 2020.

A) 2020 대통령 선거에 부정이 있었다고 트럼프 지지자들이 국회의사당을 점령하고 국회에서 각 주의 득표발표를 중단.

b) Trump 지지자들이 국회 의사당에 침입하고 투표 결과를 발표하는 2021년 1월6일 부정선거라고 투표 발표를 중단시켰다.

생활영어 정치1-3

1. The election relied on the <u>swing voters</u> in 2022.
   2022년 선거는 유동표 선거인들에게 달려 있었다.
   ** A voter who has no allegiance to any political party.

2. The <u>exit poll</u> shows the incumbent is ahead of his challenger.
   출구조사에는 현직의원 도전자보다 앞서있다.
   ** A poll taken of a sample of voters as they leave a polling place.

3. The <u>slush fund</u> is a big problem in Korean politics.
   비자금은 한국정치에 큰 문제이다.
   ** Money that is kept for dishonest or illegal activities in politics or business.

4. Many Republicans claim the 2020 election was <u>rigged.</u>
   많은 공화당 지지자는 2020년 선거가 조작됐다고 주장한다.
   ** To control or affect in a dishonest way in order to get a desired result.

5. Violent shoving matches take place once in a while between rival legislators in South Korea.
   한국에서 반대 정당 사이에 종종 험한 몸싸움이 벌어진다.
   ** To push or put in a rough, careless, or hasty manner.

6. The airport for the small town is a pure white elephant.
   그 작은 마을에 비행장 (건설이란) 빛 좋은 개살구다. [허울 좋은]
   ** Something that is costly to maintain or is incredibly hideous to the owner.

7. The government is digging out any skeletons in the closet of the oil firm to punish its outrageous profit increase.
   정부는 정유회사의 엄청난 이익금 증가를 처벌하려고 회사의 숨겨진 비리를 찾고있다.
   ** A hidden shame.

8. When it comes to their own salary increase, congress reaches bipartisan agreement in no time.
   월급 인상이라면 국회는 금방 양당이 합의가 된다.
   ** Involving the agreement or cooperation of two political parties

9. Congress turned a deaf ear when the nuclear plant was flexing its muscles to block publishing an accident of radiation leakage.
   핵발전소가 방사선 유출 사고를 언론보도에서 막으려 힘자랑하는데 국회는 못 들은척하였다.
   ** Show off one's strength or power.
   ** Turn a deaf ear: 못 들은 척하다.

10. The environmental activists lost their temper when the Fed glossed over the radiation leakage.
    환경운동가들은 정부가 방사선 유출사건을 덮어버리자 분노하였다.
    ** To hide under a deceptively attractive surface.
    ** Lose one's temper. 분노가 터지다.

11. Journalists demanded the president must come clean on who took bribes to construct the airport.
    언론인들은 공항을 세우려고 뇌물을 받은 사람이 누구인지 밝히라고 대통령에게 요구하였다.
    **To tell the truth about something.

12. Only profession becoming successful is politicians by <u>blowing His or her own horn</u>.
    자기 자랑하고 성공하는 직종은 단지 정치가들이다.
    ** Boast about one's abilities or achievements.

13. Nancy Pelosi <u>held rein</u> as house speaker in the 2010s.
    낸시는 하원의장으로 2010s에 하원을 <u>선도하였다</u>.
    ** To control.

14. The ex-president <u>went off deep end</u> when his supporters turned their back.
    전 대통령은 그의 지지자들이 등을 돌리자 <u>제정신이 아니었다</u>.
    ** To become irrational (crazy). Lose control.

15. Candidates are running around to <u>sweep</u> the slush fund <u>under the rug</u> when the election was over.
    선거가 끝나자 출마자들은 비자금을 <u>감추려</u> 뛰어다닌다.
    ** To hide something.

16. Mr Bush became a <u>lame duck</u> president when he came near the end of his term.
    부시는 2번째 임기가 끝날 즈음 <u>아무 일을 할 수 없게 되었다</u>.
    ** An elected official whose time in an office or position will soon end.

17. The citizens <u>took to the street</u> for freedom against the dictator.
    시민들은 독재자에게서 자유를 찾으려 <u>시위하러 거리로 나섰다</u>.
    ** To gather together in the public streets to show communal solidarity in either celebration or opposition.

생활영어 정치1-4

1. The candidates <u>sling mud</u> at each other from the start.
   출마자들은 처음부터 상대방의 흉허물로 공격한다.
   ** Say false or bad things about someone.

2. Trump called it a <u>witch hunt</u> when FBI searched his property to find secret government papers in 2022.
   FBI가 트럼프 집에서 2022년 국가기밀서류를 찾자 트럼프는 정치적 목적으로 (자기를 공격하러) 자기 집을 수색한다고 하였다.
   ** The searching out and deliberate harassment of those(such as political opponents).

3. The US government <u>flip-flopped</u> its relationship with Cuba.
   미국 정부는 쿠바와 (외교) 관계가 <u>변덕스러웠다.</u>
   ** Make an abrupt reversal of decision.

4. The US and China were in <u>tit-for-tat</u> sanctions on the eve of major diplomatic meeting.
   미국과 중국은 중요한 외교회의 전날 저녁에 (무역) 제재로 <u>티격태격</u>하였다.
   ** Retaliation in return for an injury from another.

5. The reporter said Trump's sex story was <u>straight from the horse's mouth.</u>
   트럼프의 섹스 이야기는 <u>직접 아는 사람에게서 들은</u> 이야기라고 기자가 말하였다.
   ** From a person who has direct personal knowledge of it.

6. The president's <u>way or the highway</u> made congress furious.
   대통령이 자기 (의견)대로 하거나 아니면 그만두라는 식에 국회는 분노하였다.
   **You either conform to their rules or leave(hit the road).

7. The defense project was over $ 13 billion in <u>pork barrel</u> spending in 2007.
   2007년 <u>선거자금 후원자에게 이권</u>(특혜)으로 국방부 프로젝트에서 130억 불이 넘었다.
   ** Benefit for fund contributor(선거자금 지원한 기업에 주는 특혜)

8. Two parties rarely see eye to eye when it comes to the defense project.
   두 정당은 국방 프로젝트가 있으면 거의 의견이 다르다.
   ** Agree.

9. Voters see the glass as half empty; others see it as half full.
   유권자들은 남의 잔이 반이 비어 있다고 하나, 다른 사람들은 유리잔이 50%가 채워졌다고 본다.
   ** 유리잔에 물이 50% 채워졌다고 주장할 수도 있고, 반대당은 50%가 비었다고 주장한다.

10. The tongue-in-cheek remark was not meant to be taken seriously, but Sarah was easily offended.
    아이러니한 카멘트는 심각하게 받아들이지 말아야 했는데 Sarah의 반응은 불쾌하게 받아드렸다.
    ** To speak ironically or mockingly; slyly insincere.

11. Some of the power holders in Arab nations are not interested In disrupting the status quo.
    아랍국가들의 일부 권력자들은 현 상태(왕국제도)를 바꾸면서 교란시킬 흥미가 없다.
    ** An existing state of affairs.

12. Minority parties closed ranks to defeat the ruling party's new bill.
    야당들은 여당의 새 안건을 부결하려고 단합하였다.
    ** To stay united.

13. Burma's citizens are fed up with military government.
    미얀마 시민들은 군부정권에 진저리를 낸다.
    ** Disgusted with someone or something.

Find an unfit word

A. During the campaign, the candidates lied _____ .
   ① left and right ② through his teeth ③ brazenly ④ thoroughly

B. The candidate refused to stop _____ his opponent.
   ① beating ② blasting ③ knockinging ④ sniping

*** Answer: A-④, B-④

🔍 미국의 두 정당 position

공화당(코끼리, 적색, GOP): 친기업, 친총기 소유, 백인 지지율 높음. 기업을 지원하고 남쪽지역과 중부지역 백인들이 많이 이 정당을 지지한다. 사회복지 지원 정책보다 국방력 강조.

민주당(당나귀, 청색): 친-노조, 낙태승인, 총기 소유 반대, 소수민족 지원, 사회복지 강조, LGBT 지지.

** LGBT: lesbian, gay, bisexual, and transgender

🔍 〈선거자금 조직〉 PAC: Political Action Committee.

정치 출마자를 위해 선거자금 모으는 미국 단체. 재벌의 큰 선거 자금은 공화당에 많이 지원하는 편이다. 2024년 대통령 선거에 테슬라 회사의 머스크는 선거자금 $288 million을 트럼프에게 지원.

🔍 도미노 정책(Domino Theory)과 월남전쟁

한 국가가 공산국이 되면 연쇄적으로 주변 국가들이 공산화된다는 주장을 앞세운 미국은 월남전을 시작하고, 미국의 청년들은 반정부 시위를 일으키고, 미국 국민들이 정치에 가담하기 시작하였다.

President Lyndon Johnson believed in the "domino theory," the idea that when one country becomes communist then surrounding countries will also fall under communist influence. After he was elected president of the United States, Johnson sent the first American combat troops to Vietnam in Feb. 1965. Although his domestic policies received high approval ratings from the American public, his popularity declined because of his administration's hawkish approach to the Vietnam Crisis.

Perhaps most notable were the protests prior to and during the 1968 Democratic National Convention. These protests led to a federal investigation, and eight demonstrators (known as the Chicago Eight, later Seven) were famously charged with conspiring to use interstate commerce with intent to Incite a riot.

Chicago History museum

🔍 미국의 2020 대통령 선거의 비리

On January 6, 2021, following the defeat of U.S. President Donald Trump in the presidential election, a crowd of his supporters attacked the United States Capitol Building in Washington, D.C. The crowd sought to keep Trump in power by preventing a joint session of Congress from Counting The Electoral College. <Capital Attract. Jan. 6, 2021 Wikipedia>

From the perspective of the former president, the attack on the Capitol was the result of an election that he falsely says was stolen. Trump claims the attackers were mere protesters, falsely maligned by the media and his opponents. <by Washington Post>

The Jan. 6 attack on the Capitol: A guide to what we now know –

The 2020 presidential election was not fair, and no honest a person would claim that it was. The system was rigged against one candidate and in favor of another, and not in ways that were hidden... <by Fox News>

Tucker Carlson: Yes, the election was rigged for Joe Biden. Here's how | Fox News

It was a phone call Brad Raffensperger will never forget. For more than an hour last winter, then-President Donald Trump rattled off false claim after false claim about dead people voting and absentee-ballot fraud, culminating in a now famoouse request to Raffensperger, Georgia's Republican secretary of state: "Find 11,780 votes." Raffensperger declined. Mr. President, the challenge that you have is the data you have is wrong Raffensperger said. <by NPR>

🔍 Ex-president Trump

Jan. 6, 2021.

"We're going to the Capitol," he says. "We're going to try and give them [Republicans] the kind of pride and boldness that they need to take back our country." Said Trump.

맥카티즘 - McCarthyism

이차대전 이후 공산국을 적대하는 풍토를 업고 국회의원 조셉 맥카티는 자기의 반대당이나 의견이 다른 국가 공무원들이 공산당 의심이 간다고 수사를 하면서 권력을 가지다가 그의 수단에 분노하여 국회에서 추방당했다.

한국도 군부 박정희, 전두환, 심지어 윤석열 정부도 이 수단을 썼는지 의심이 간다.

In 1953, congressman Joseph McCarthy was put in charge of the Committee on Government Operations, which allowed him to launch even more expansive investigations of the alleged communist infiltration of the federal government. In hearing after hearing, he aggressively interrogated witnesses in what many came to perceive as a blatant violation of their civil rights. Despite a lack of any proof of subversion, more than 2,000 government employees lost their jobs as a result of McCarthy's investigations.

Chapter 20-3.

정치 - 사법부

Politics – Judiciary

생활영어   사법부

1. The **appellate court** overturned the circuit court's decision.
   고등법원은 지방법원의 판결을 번복하였다.

2. The assailant committed **felonies** twice before.
   가해자는 전에도 두 번 중범죄를 범했다.

3. The judge sentenced **capital punishment** to the terrorist.
   판사는 테러인에게 사형을 선고하였다.

4. The policeman **took the withness stand** to show the situation.
   경찰은 상황을 보여주려 증언대에 섰다.

5. The city hall announced the city will **weed out** drug dealers.
   시청은 마약범을 뿌리뽑겠다고 발표하였다.
   ** To get rid of people or things that are not wanted.

6. The suspect **turned himself in.**
   그 범인은 자수하였다.
   ** To give or return something or someone to an authority.

7. The prosecutor **left no stone unturned** to find hard evidence for months.
   증거를 찾으려 검찰은 샅샅이 찾았다.
   ** To do everything you can to achieve a good result.

8. Saudi Arabia set to **bend its rule** to allow Ronaldo to live with his girlfriend.
   사우디아라비아는 호날두(축구선수)가 애인과 동거생활 하도록 허락하여 법을 어기게 하였다. [사우디는 결혼 안 하고 동거를 금지시킴]
   ** To do something which is not normally allowed.

9. The defense attorney claims his client hasn't <u>a shred of evidence</u>.
   피고의 변호사는 그가 <u>작은 증거</u> 하나도 없다고 주장한다.
   ** The slightest bit of evidence or proof.

10. The thief saw the cop approaching but managed to <u>give the policeman the slip</u>.
    그 도둑은 경찰이 오는 것을 보고 경찰을 <u>빠져나갔다(따돌렸다)</u>.
    ** To escape.

Find an unfit word

A. The city closed down 12 restaurants that violated the city _____ .
   ① code ② constitution ③ law ④ ordinance

B. The CEO attempted to _____ the company money for his personal gain.
   ① divert ② funnel ③ misuse ④ replenish

*** Answer: A-②, B-④

생활영어 법률

1. The defendant decided to cop a plea in order to get a lighter sentence.
   그 피고는 감형을 받으려 죄를 인정하였다.
   ** To admit fault and plead for mercy.

2. The defendant jumped bail and left the city.
   피고는 보석금을 내고 재판장에 나오지 않고 어디로 도주하였다.
   ** To fail to appear for a court appearance after depositing (posting) bail.

3. The policeman gave benefit of the doubt when the guy said he did not hit the car.
   그 차를 부딪치지 않았다고 말하자 경찰은 의심이 가지만 그의 말을 믿어주었다.
   ** To accept what a person says as true even though you may feel skeptical about what they are saying.

4. The FBI sifted the spy property with a fine tooth comb to find government documents.
   FBI는 정부서류를 찾으려 간첩의 건물을 샅샅이 뒤졌다.
   ** sift with a fine tooth comb. check very careful and thorough.

5. The judge said he was willing to let plaintiff have his day in court again.
   판사는 원고에게 말할(변명?) 기회를 다시 줄 의사가 있다고 말했다.
   ** Have an opportunity to be heard.

6. 300 dollars fine was a slap on the wrist for the huge building damage.
   큰 건물 파손에 300불 벌금은 솜방망이 처벌이다.
   ** Mild punishment(경미한 처벌)

7. The store manager made a federal case when a customer broke the circular saw blade at the hardware store.
   고객이 전기 톱날을 부수자 철물점 매니저는 손님이 대형사고를 낸 것처럼 만들었다.

** to exaggerate the importance of something.

8. The suspect eventually came clean on his crime.
   범인은 결국 그의 범죄를 실토하였다.
   ** keep nothing hidden.

9. The assailant hid in a basement until the coast was clear.
   가해자는 (경찰이) 사라질 때까지 지하실에서 숨어 있었다.
   ** Someone can go somewhere or do something without being caught or seen.

10. The Banking Committee's loophole is so big that a bonus-ridden AIG trucks can make a U-turn.
    은행분과 위원회의 허점(탈출구)이 너무 커서 보너스를 실은 AIG 트럭이 U-turn을 할 수 있을 만큼 크다.
    ** 허점(탈출구멍)

Find an incorrect word

A. The criminal made a _____ company to hide drug business.
   ① dummy ② front ③ paper ④ shell

B. The prosecutor had to submit _____ evidence to the court.
   ① concrete ② forensic ③ hard ④ substantial

C. FBI agents _____ Colombian's drug shipments at the airport.
   ① confiscated ② dispatched ③ impounded ④ seized

D. Investigators say that Mr. Roberts had planed the murder to _____ get life insurance money.
   ① itenary ② plot ③ scam ④ scheme

*** Answer. A-③, B-④, C-②, D-①

Chapter 20-3. 정치 - 사법부 | 213

Pick an incorrect Word

A. Any big firm's _____ was not jailed for price-fixing or monopoly in Mexico.

　① hancho　② kingpin　③ ring leader　④ top notch

B. 16% of people used _____ Social Security numbers and false addresses to obtain Federal assistance aids after Cobid-19 disaster.

　① fictitious　② fraudulent　③ hypothetical　④ phony

C. The contract shall be _____ because the seller falsified Goods they promised to send.

　① nullified　② void　③ invalidated　④ stalled

D. The Russian spy has been traveling Europe nations with a _____ passport.

　① bogus　② delinquent　③ fake　④ forged

　　　　　　　　　　　　　*** Answer: A-④, B-③, C-④, D-②

Corruption in the judiciary of Cook County

Operation Greylord in Chicago area

　미국 시카고 지역(郡, Cook County) 법정의 비리 FBI와 국세청(IRS)은 1980s년 3년 8개월 수사로 17명의 판사와 48명의 변호사, 법무부 직원을 합하여 92명을 기소하였다.

　마피아와 관련된 수사가 많았고, 판사 Maloney는 3건의 살인 사건을 덮어주고 100,00불을 받아 16년 감옥에 살다가 출옥하고 같은 해 사망하였다. 미국 역사상 제일 큰 법무부 스캔들이었다.

미국 변호사협회, American Bar Assoc.

WEB Jul 14, 2015 In 1980, Terrence Hake was a young to assist the FBI and the United States Attorney's Office in an investigation of the County court system, known nationwide to be a hotbed of bribery, corruption, and mob ties.

Operation Greylord: The True Story of an Untrained Undercover Agent and America's Biggest Corruption Bust (americanbar.org)

WEB Mar 10, 2023 · When the last Greylord trial concluded in 1994, Hake testified at the trials of 23 defendants. Hake is a graduate of Loyola University of Chicago School of Law. He started as a prosecutor in the Cook County State's Attorney's Office where he noticed and reported corruption in the court process. He served in federal law enforcement for...

미국 법무부, U.S. Department of Justice

WEB To that end, important recommendations have been Made (some of which have already been implemented) to reform the administration of justice in Cook County, adopt new ethical requirements for judges and attorneys, and allow merit selection of judges in Illinois. As in all corruption cases, There is at least one important lesson to be derived ...

Operation Greylord and Its Aftermath | Office of Justice Programs (ojp.gov)

Chapter 21.
아랍국가의 독재자 후세인

Hussein, the dictator of an Arab country

에덴동산이라고 불리던 고대문명지 메소포타미아의 티그리스 강과 유프라테스 강의 물줄기를 바꿔(divert) 독재자 후세인은 그 문명을 파괴하였다.

BC 3100년 Mesopotamia 문명이 형성된 이라크의 늪 지역. 주민들이 후세인의 폭정으로 2006년 고향을 버렸다.

이라크의 후세인은 자기를 추종하지 않는 국민들을 제거하려고 세계 문명의 발상지인 메소포타미아(Mesopotamia, 3,100 BC) 유프라데스 강(euphrates river)과 티그리스강 강물을 새 수로를 만든 곳으로 물길을 돌려(divert) 기독교의 에덴동산으로도 알려진 지역을 폐허로 만들었다. 후세인(Sadam Hussein)은 이라크 대통령으로 24년 통치 중 두 번 전쟁을 일으켜 백만여 명의 인구가 사망하고, 300만여 명의 국민이 국가를 버리고 $561 billion의 국가 재산을 소모하였다. 미국의 부시 대통령은 특수부대로 후세인을 체포하여 재판으로 사형을 시켰다.

🔍 United States Institute of Peace

published by the Brookings Institution and the School of Advanced International Studies at Johns Hopkins University. Oct. 2002. In the early 1990s, in a vicious campaign to root out rebels hiding in the marshes, Iraq's then-president Saddam Hussein diverted the Tigris and Euphrates rivers, and burned and poisoned the land. The devastation has not been the result of a direct assault on the people themselves, but on the environment that was the foundation of their existence—the marshlands

Covering about 12,000 square miles recently as 1985, the three contiguous marshes have been drained, burned and damned to the point that only remnants of them still exist..

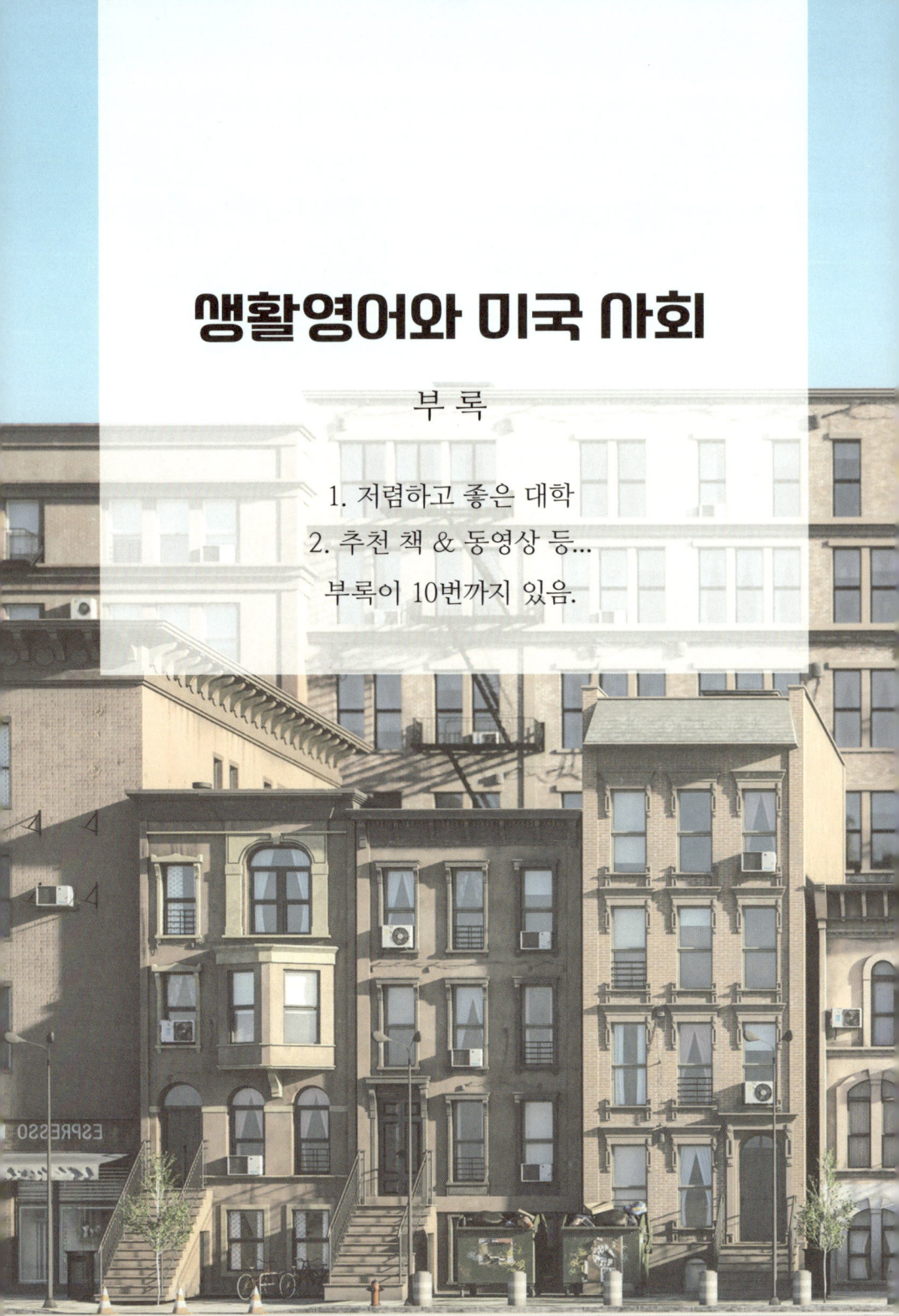

생활영어와 미국 사회

부 록

1. 저렴하고 좋은 대학
2. 추천 책 & 동영상 등...
부록이 10번까지 있음.

1. 미국의 좋은 주립대학 50학교

평균 1년 주립대학 등록금은 $ 12,000~ 18,000 이지만 서민 연봉으로 명문 사립대 보내기 힘들어 돈을 빌린다. 우리집 둘째는 졸업한지 10년이 지났는데도 은행빚이 $ 120,000불이 남았다.

〈CBS-TV & US News 추천한 50개 주립대학 & SAT 점수2023〉

(사립 명문대 대부분은 입학 SAT는 1,500이 넘는다.)

no.	학 교	State	School 일년 등록금	SAT	학생수
1	UCLA	CA. Los Angeles	$ 16,474	1,570	40.6k
2	Univ. of Michigan	Mich-Ann Arbor	$ 17,832	1,470	51.2k.
3	Georgia Inst. of Tech	Atlanta	$ 17,410	1,470	14.7k
4	Univ. of Virginia	VA-Charlottesville	$ 19,043	1,530	
5	US Military-West Point	N.Y	$ 0	1,350	
6	Univ. of Florida	Fl.-Gainesville	$ 10,075	1,400	
7	Univ. of N. Carolina	Chapel Hill	$ 10,038	1,415	
8	Univ. of Texas	TX-Austine	$ 16,892	1,370	
9	Univ. Of Calf	Calf Berkeley	$ 19,329	1,570	
10	Univ. of Georgia	GA.-Athens	$ 16,580	1,310	27.8K
11	Univ. of Wisconsin	WI- Madison	$ 14,030	1,440	30.0K
12	Univ of Illinois	IL, Urbana S	$ 13,517	1,440	31.1K
13	Florida State Univ	FL-Tallahassee	$ 12,815	1,270	29.0K
14	College of William & M,VA	Williamsburg	$ 18,588	1,520	
15	Penn State Univ.	PA - Abington	$ 26,151	1,380	
16	Univ of Calf. Irvine. Calf		$ 13,106	1,332	
17	Virginia Tech	VA-Blackburge	$ 20,247	1,330	
18	Univ. of Washing-ton-WA-Seattle		$ 9,661	1,420	29.3k

no.	학교	State	School 일년 등록금	SAT	학생수
19	Texas A&M Univ.	TX— Aggie	$ 19,906	1,270	
20	Univ. Calf.-San Diago	Calf	$ 15,222	1,370	
21	Purdue Univ.	Indiana — W. Lafayett	$ 12,294	1,315	33.5k
22	Ohio State Univ.	OH.— Columbus	$ 18,884	1,340	43.0k
23	N. Carolina State Univ.	SC.— Raleigh	$ 14,600		23.0k
24	Univ.of Calf. — Davis	Calf. — Davis	$ 17,026	1,270	30k
25	Univ. of Calf — Santa Barbara	Santa Barbara,calf—S.B.	$ 17,223	1,355	22k
26	Univ of Pittsburgh	PA, Pittsburgh	$ 22,346	1,370	
27	Univ.of Minnesota	Minneapolis	$ 17,729	1,378	
28	Colorado School of Mines		$ 27,675		
29	Univ. of S. Florida	Fl. Tampa	$ 10,004	1,325	
30	Univ. of Maryland	College Park	$ 17,643	1,380	
31	Michigan State Univ.	E. Lansing	$ 16,655	1,220	
32	Clemson Univ.	S.C—Clemson	$ 22,935	1,320	20k
33	Rutgers Univ.	N.J —New Brunswick	$ 17,835	1,295	33.7k
34	Oklahoma State Univ.	Ok. Stillwater	$ 14,763	1,160	
35	Indiana Univ.	IN—Bloomington	$ 13,191	1,280	
36	Michigan Tech Univ.	Houghton	$ 17,356	1,231	
37	Univ. of Massachusetts —Amherst		$ 22,505	1,370	22.2k
38	Univ. of C. Florida	Orlando	$ 11,108	1,360	43.0k
39	Univ. of Iowa	Iowa City	$ 17,452	1,240	20.0k
40	Univ. of Utah	Salt lake City	$ 12,881	1,280	18.7k
41	Univ. of Alabama	Birmingham	$ 16,978	1,210	
42	Arizona State Univ.	Tempe	$ 14,653	1,245	57k
43	U.S. Merchant Marine	N.Y. Kings point	$ 4,574	1,310	
44	Florida Int'l Univ.	FL. Miami	$ 8,988	1,159	24k

no.	학교	State	School 일년 등록금	SAT	학생수
45	Univ. of Cincinnati	Ohio, Cincinnati	$ 22,767	1,170	
46	Iowa State Univ.	Iowa-Ames	$ 16,105	1,220	24k
47	Univ. of Mississippi	Oxford	$ 13,540	1,134	
48	Auburn Univ.	Alabama, Auburn	$ 24,028		
49	Univ. Of S. Carolina	S.C. Columbia	$ 21,784	1,245	26k
50	Univ. of Oklahoma	OK-Norman	$ 21,836	1,210	18k

50개 수준 낮은 대학 명단- MSN: Microsoft가 발표
2023년 The 50 Worst Colleges In America Ranked- MSn

2. 교재

듣는 교재: 1.5세부터 우리 집 아이들이 보고 들을 때 교재는 만화 영화이다. TV나 인터넷의 만화를 1시간만 보라고 해도 끄지 않고 본다. 끄지 말라고 애원한다. 이렇게 영어 배우겠다고 애원하는 교재가 영어 만화 교재이다.

2시간 영어 만화 보면 학원 보내지 않고 미국, 영국 아이들처럼 한국 시골 아이들도 영어를 잘한다. 우리 집 아이들은 1.5세부터 하루에 2시간씩 허락해 주었다. 제일 무서운 벌이 2시간 TV, 인터넷 보지 못하는 벌이다. 영어 ABC 몰라도 그림 보고 내용과 뜻을 알아낸다.

<한국 부모들의 제일 큰 실수가 영어 만화 교재를 모른다.>

** 우리 집 소라, 아리아, 아렉스도 더 보자고 1.5세부터 애원한 아이들이다.

1. Finding Nemo
2. Toy Story
3. Monsters, Inc.
4. Inside Out

위의 만화는 2년 정도 계속 보던 만화이다.

부모들이 영어를 안 하니 듣지 못하는데, 이 만화는 영어 듣기 최고의 교재. 듣지 못하면 말도 잘 못합니다. 1.5세부터 시작합시다. 못 알아듣는다고 걱정하는데 그림으로 말의 뜻을 찾아낸다. 6개월 지나면 아이들이 부모의 말을 이해하고 알아듣기 시작한다.

초등 3~5학년 학교에서 추천하는 책, 상받은 책

이때 미국 학생 읽는 속도가 107~194 단어(60초)

Missing May	By 〈 Cynthia Rylan 〉
Sarah, Plain and Tall.	By 〈 P. MacLachlan 〉
Bridge to Terabithia.	By 〈 K. Paterson 〉
Jacob Have I loved?	By 〈 K. Paterson 〉
Seed Falks.	By 〈Paul Fleischman.〉
Freckle Juice.	By 〈Judy Blume 〉
Flat Stanley.	By 〈 Jeff Brown 〉
Tales of a 4th grader Nothing.	By 〈 Judy Blume 〉
Out of The dust	By 〈 Karen Hesse 〉
The Mouse and Motorcycle.	By 〈 B. Clearly 〉

** 남아들 3~4학년들이 즐겨 읽음. 이 시리즈로 2권이 있음

The Boxcar Children.	By 〈Gertrude Warner〉

영화도 나오고 시리즈도 많이 나왔음.

이 나이가 아주 중요한 시간이다. 3~5학년 때가 부모가 시키는 말을 듣고 5학년에게 무엇을 시키면 피해 다니는 학생들이 많다. 한국 학생들에게 영어 책을 읽어주면 5분 이상 듣지 않는 학생들이 80% 이상이다. 재미나고 쉬운 책으로 1분당(60초) 120~150단어 읽고 이해하는 것이 미국 초등학교 4, 5학년 수준이다.

TV 기자들이 60초에 150~170단어를 말한다.

추천하는 유아교재는 1980s년부터 3대째 우리 집에서 읽어주던 classic 책, Caldecott, Newbery medal, Horn Book, ALA 수상작가 이외 인기 높은 Judy Blume, B. Cleary, young adult 작가 Paterson 등입니다.

이 책들은 도서관, 미국 초등학교에서 숙제로 읽을 책들이며 독후감에 (Book report) 사용하는 책들이다.

중학생 & up 추천책

To Kill a Mockingbird	By 〈Harper Lee〉
Holes by	By 〈Louis Sachar〉
Lord of the Flies	By 〈William Golding〉
The Call of the Wild	By 〈Jack London〉
Wolf Hall	By 〈Hilary Mantel〉
Outsiders	By 〈S. E. Hinton〉
The One and Only Ivan	By 〈Katherine Applegate〉
Liddy	BY 〈Katherine Paterson〉
The Picture of Dorian Grey	BY 〈Oscar Wild〉
The Grapes of Wrath	By 〈John Steinback〉
One flew over the Cuckoo's Nest	By 〈Ken Kesey〉

미국 학생 읽는 속도

초등 3학년	107~ 148 단어(60초에, WPM)
중학생(11~14살)	150 ~ 204
고등학생(14세~18세)	200 ~300
대학생(18세~23세)	300 ~ 350
성 인	220~ 350

읽는 속도 격차는 눈으로 읽는 방법, 소리 내 읽는 속도, 도시와 시골, 저 소득층, 여자와 남자에 따라서 30~50 읽는 단어 속도가 벌어집니다.

〈언론사 기자 발음 속도: 150 ~170단어. 60초에〉

3, 4살 되면 책을 못 읽어도 잘 듣고 부모와 말도 잘하기 시작하며 농담, 과장, 변명도 할 능력이 생깁니다. 언어는 두 종류의 다른 공부입니다. 문맹자가 책은 읽지 못해도 말은 잘하는 시골 아저씨, 할머니들이 있습니다. 한국 학교

는 머릿속에서 문장 만드는 연습을 시키지 않았습니다. 그러니 한국 학생들이 고등학교 다녀도 머릿속에서 영어로 문장을 만들어 대화를 하지 못합니다. 마치 키보드(key board)를 보지 않고는 타이프를 못 치는 것과 같습니다.

문장을 만들어 본 적이 없어서 고등학생들이 외국인들과 잘 대화를 못 하며, 1분에 150단어 대화하는 뉴스 역시 잘 듣지 못 합니다.

** 미국 아이들은 2, 3살 때부터 문장을 머리에서 만들고 말하기 시작합니다. 우리 집은 유아부터 초등학교 2학년까지 취침 전 30~60분 책을 읽어주었는데, 고맙게도 무료로 Youtube에서 명작(classic) 책들을 듣고 읽은 동영상 책들을 올려주었습니다.

"Thank you so much, YouTube!"
한 한국 출판사 직원은 이런 것 다 학원에서 배운다고 멍청하게 말하는 소리를 들었습니다.

유아 때부터~초등 2학년까지 우리 집에서 읽어주고 있는 classic 책이 YouTube에서 무료로 듣고, 보고, 읽을 수 있는 책으로 3대째 이어온 책들인데 요사이 6세의 Mason이 말을 못 한다고 2살 Aria에게 읽어줍니다.

1. Are you my Mother ? 〈by P D Eastman〉 5분 16초.
Are You My Mother? By P.D. Eastman Read Aloud (youtube.com)

2. Harry the Dirty Dog 〈by G. Zion〉 4분6초.
HARRY the Dirty Dog – Read Aloud Funny Stores (youtube.com)

3. The Hungry Caterpillar 〈E. Carle〉 4분30초.
The Very Hungry Caterpillar by Eric Carle Read Aloud (youtube.com)

4. The Three Little Pigs 〈5분〉
The Three Little Pigs – Read aloud in fullscreen with music and sound effects! (youtube.com)

5. Ms. Nelson is missing 〈H. Allard & J. Marshall〉 5분
Miss Nelson Is Missing – Book Read Aloud (youtube.com)

6. Martha Speaks 〈by S. Meddaugh〉10분
MARTHA SPEAKS by Susan Meddaugh : Kids Books Read Aloud (youtube.com)

인기가 많아 TV연재로 나왔으니 원본 책을 찾아야함.

7. Curious George 〈By H.A. Rey〉 7분 33초
THE ORIGINAL CURIOUS GEORGE by H.A. Rey – Books for Children Read Aloud! (youtube.com)

이 이야기는 시시한 것(silly)인데 유아들은 흥미 있는 모양. 이 silly 책이 연재로 30여 권 되는 것 같습니다.

한국 부모들의 영어 교육 제언

2살부터 만화 동영상을 TV에서 하루에 2시간씩 듣고 보는 방법이 제일 중요하며 못 알아들어도 그림으로 혼자 뜻을 알아듣습니다. You Tube에 많이 있음. 두 살부터는 말은 못해도 영어를 알아듣고 심부름을 영어로 시키면 알아듣고 심부름합니다.
이때부터 유아들은 영어 만화를 중단시킬 때까지 지켜봅니다.
이런 좋은 기회를 한국 부모들은 모두 놓치고 있습니다.
영어를 쓰지 않는 한국에는 영어를 배우는 최고가 만화입니다. 우리 집 소라는 "Finding Nimo"를 1.5세부터 매일 두어 번씩 보았음. 현우는(Alex) ABC 책을 공부하자고 하면 듣지도 않고 PBS-TV를 매일 두어 시간 보았습니다. 시원찮은 교재도 안 보고 학원도 보내지 않고 자기가 동영상 만화로 혼자 영어를 배워서 유치원에서 단어 실력이 제일 많은 유치원 학생 중의 한 명이었습니다.
우리 집 사촌까지 포함해서 한국말을 제일 잘하는 3세는 사촌 집 어머니가 한국 연속극 볼 때 옆에서 같이 본 조카가 한국말을 제일 잘한다. 우리 집은 일주일에 한 시간씩 두세 번 가르쳤는데 실패해서 연세대 여름방학에 보냈는데 실패하였다.
석진과 유진은 미국에 태어났어도 할머니와 자라서 영어를 못 했는데 유치원 들어가서 2학년 때는 한국말을 잊어버렸다.

제일 많이 보는 만화나 동영상

현우(Alex)는 Thomas & Friends(PBS-TV, 2~4살) 하루에 두어 시간을 보고 영어공부 하자고 해도 피해다니며 Leap Frog로 영어를 배운 경우이다. 그러나 현우가 영어는 거의 만점을 받았다.

Thomas & Friends 시리즈(동영상)

1984년~ 2021년 PBS-TV가 37년간 584편을 만들어 8천800만여 명의 아이들이 본 초대형 시리즈임.

우리 집 5명, 3세까지 본 미국 국영방송에서 보여줌.

***   ***   ***

어머니가 직장 다니는 유아들이 듣는 연습은 TV-PBS, Youtube가 가르치고 있다고 말해도 되는데, 한국은 학교에서 시원찮은 선생, 시원찮은 책으로 돈을 주고 영어듣기를 배운다면 돈과 시간을 낭비하고 있는 결과이다.

우리 집 Baby Sitters들(멕시코 사람)은 영어를 잘못해서 동영상 영어 만화를 하루에 2-3시간 TV에서 듣는다. 자기 전 30분 내지 한 시간 6살까지 유아 책들을 매일 읽어주었다. 3가지 언어를 듣던 아이들이라 다른 아이들보다 영어가 6개월~18개월 정도 늦게 말했다.

〈동영상 만화영화 교재〉

아마 이 교재가 부모들이 영어를 쓰지 않는 한국 학생들이 영어 배우는 가장 중요한 역할을 한다고 말할 수 있습니다.

🔍 3. 연령별, 교육별 단어 차이(책 선택 참고 위해서)

유아 단어		수능시험		collogual, Slang
실수	boo-boo	injury		XXXX.
아픔	ouch	affliction		XXX
상처	owie	injury, pain		XXX
엉덩이	behind	buttock	ass, rear end. Fanny.	
멍청이	dumb	Imbecile		knucklehead, pin head numb suckle, meat head
Xxxxxxxxxx		snap	freak out	
더러운	Yucky	disgusting		gross
소변보다		pee	Urinate	piss, take a leak.
잡담하다		chat	prattle	shoot the breeze, chew the
비위 맞추다		xxx	flatter	Kiss one's butt. brown nose
작살내다		crush	devastate	Kick one's ass

친구 Allen의 wife에게 "up your ass."에 맞는 번역을 내가 못 찾았다니까 한국에서 중학교 졸업한 그 한국계 wife가 "엿먹어라."라고 말해줬다. Chicago Sun Time 일간지에 죄수들이 쓰는 단어, 운송업 직원들 단어들을 우리 회사 직원들에게 물었더니 30~35%는 모른다고 하였다.

🔍 4. 한글과 영어단어 다른 점

기초단어에서 한글은 한 단어로 쓰는데 영어는 두 단어로 쓰는 단어들을 초등학생들에게 부모나 선생님들이 알려 주어야 말하거나 문장 만들 때 큰 도움이 된다.

한글은 한 단어로 이어 쓰는데 영어는 두 단어로 사용함

〈예문〉

길다 ➡ 긴+이다 long + is < Train is long >
무겁다 ➡ 무거운+이다 Heavy + is < It is heavy >
'기차는 길다' 를 번역하면 영어에 '길다' 단어가 없으니
길다 ➡ long + is로 만들어 문장을 만들어야 한다.
기차는 길다 ➡ Train is long.
애기는 예쁘다 ➡ Baby is pretty.

그래서 대화나 책을 3~5년을 공부해야 단어로 문장을 만들 수 있다.
아래 단어는 형용사+ Be동사로 바꾸어 쓰는 단어.
가렵다, 가볍다, 가늘다(굵다), 깊다(낱다. shallow)
낮다(low,높다), 넓다(좁다), 느리다(빠르다), 무겁다.
덥다(춥다), 닮다(sweet), 단단하다(sturdy), 많다,
미끄럽다, 맵다, 무섭다, 시다(sour), 쓰다(bitter), 시끄럽다,
약하다, 아프다, 외롭다, 작다(크다), 쉽다(힘들다), 졸립다,
차갑다. 뜨겁다, 피곤하다, 행복하다.
<색깔>: 노랗다, 빨갛다, 파랗다, 희다. etc…
졸립다(sleepy)는 없어도 졸다(doze)는 있다(Be 동사).

영어는 한 단어인데 한글은 두 단어

Water(물을 주다). root(뿌리를 내린다), saw(톱으로 자르다),
Flush(물을 내린다), sharpen(칼로 연필을) 날카롭게 갈다.
  ** 부모, 선생님들이 이 문제점을 학생들에게 설명해 주지 않으면 초등학생들이 문장들을 잘못 만들며 대화도 계속 틀립니다.

5. 작문과 대화 연습- 지도(map)나 그림을 대화 자료로

대화를 어떻게 하면 빨리 배울 수 있느냐고 묻는 사람을 종종 본다, 타이프 빨리 치는 법 가르쳐 달라는 질문과 같다. 1.5세부터 5살 될 때까지 유아들은 온종일 부모, 형제, 친구, TV 만화 등을 매일 10시간 이상 듣고, 보고 말한다. 한국 학생들은?

대화는 머릿속에서 문장을 만드는 일이다.
한국 학생들은 초등 3학년 때 시작하여 고등학생 되어도 작문, 대화를 한다거나 영어 대화나 tv 뉴스 듣는 기회가 적어 힘들어한다.

내가 학생들애게 칠판에 지도를 걸어주고 A에서 B로 가는 길을 영어로 설명하라고 시켰다. 90% 이상이 문장을 만들지 못하고 영국에서 살다온 학생 한 명만 만들었다.
길 하나를 영어로 말하면 다음 길을 (지도에서) 몰라 문장을 연결 못해 다음 문장을 못 만든다. 그래서 한쪽 뇌는 지도가 있고, 한쪽 뇌에서는 문장을 만든다.
타이프 키보드에 ㄱ, ㄴ, A, B, C, 단어 위치 모르면 글 쓰기 힘들듯이…
또 여러 그림을 보여주고 무슨 그림이냐고 질문하여 문장을 만들 화제를 끌어내어 보았다.
선생님이 수영하는 법 가르쳐 주어도 혼자 깊은 물에 들어가지 못하고, 자전거 배워 혼자 연습해 쓰러지지 않게 연습해야 한다.

듣기: 미국 기자들 뉴스 방송은 60초에 150~170 단어를 말하니 첫해는 무슨 단어를 발음하는지 겨우 아니까 유아 대화를 듣는다.

🔍 6. 다른 표현 & 작문 – 영어와 한글 표현이 비슷한 단어

** chew(씹다, scold, criticize)

His coach chewed the soccer player when he made a mistake.
** kill: His joke kills many fans at the TV talk show. 그의 농담은 많은 TV 관객을 (웃겨) 죽여준다.

** sweep: Our team swept the 3 games series (싹 쓸었다. 전승)

** melt: The back-rib melted in my mouth. (그 갈비는 입에서 녹았다.)

** A swan among ducks (군계일학)이나, thorn in the eye (눈의 가시)

〈아래 단어는 사회가 엉뚱한 단어를 쓴다.〉
시간을 벌다에 earn이 아니고 buy를 쓴다.

〈계약을 맺다〉에 엉뚱한 단어를 쓴다.
We reached a deal이거나…
We cut (or ink, seal, strike) a deal.
그래서 TV나 책을 많이 읽어야 영어에 쓰는 문장을 이해한다.

(시비를) 걸다에: Pick a fight.
(주먹을) 날리다: pull (or swing) a punch.
(의심이) 가다, 사다: raise doubt
(주의를) 끌다: draw attention.
(약, 법 효과가) 나다: take effect.
(판결을) 내리다: deliver sentence.
(용기) 내다: gather up courage.
(횡재) 맞다: strike a fortune.
(시간을) 벌다: buy time.
(술책) 부리다: pull a scheme(trick).
(행동을) 취하다: take an action.
(앙심을) 품다: hold grudge.

⟨Fly(파리)⟩
한글: 장사가 안될 때 "파리 날리다"
영어: 죽어갈 때(약해서?) Die like Flies
(over a short period of time in large numbers)

⟨비슷한 표현⟩
1. wash one's hand. (손씻다, 손 털다)
2. throw up one's hand. (두손 들었다, 기권)
3. tighten a belt. (허리띠를 졸라매다, 돈을 절약하다.)
4. turn one's back. (등을 돌리다, 배반).
5. 머리카락이 곤두선다.
The spooky movie has a hair raising story.
Their hair stands on end.
6. 꼬리를 내리고: with tail between one's legs.
7. 안경 쓴 사람(목사): four eyes
8. 배 아파함(질투 때문에) : belly ache.
9. 큰집(교도소): big house.
10. 돈세탁: money laundry
11. 육감: sixth sense
12. 나사가 빠지다: He's got a screw loose.
13. 사탕발림: sugar coating.
14. 눈더미처럼 불어나다: snowball (돈 이자)
15. 혀를 차다: cluck.

7. 다르게 사용하는 단어

오픈-카	convertible.
캠핑카	recreation vehicle(R.V.)
핸들	steering wheel.
백미러	rear-view mirror.
오토바이	motor cycle.
샤프(연필)	mechanical pencil.
스탠드	lamp with stand.
아이쇼핑	window shopping.
러닝머신	tread mill.
보닛	hood(bonnet은 한국에서 들은 단어)

8. 부사– 편리하게 쓸 수 있는 부사절

⟨At⟩
We bought it at a low price.
Swim at your own risk.
Meet you at the meeting.

⟨시간, 장소⟩
at dawn, at evening, at night,
at home, at school, at café and so on.

⟨For⟩
The store sells it for $ 6 dollars.
He is late for the train.
We tease him for fun.

⟨In⟩
The Patient is in danger after a surgery.
Voters were in doubt about the candidate's promise.
We are in favor of lower tax.
We wait for him in hope to meet in person.

The church helps poor people in need.
The patient is in pain.
The negotiation is in progress.
He gave us a ride. In return, we bought him dinner.
Debris found in search for a missing airplane.

〈시간〉 in April (to December), year, in decade, in century.
〈장소〉 in London, county, China(nation), world.

〈On〉
Howl of Wolves put the sheeps on alert.
Put the coffee on the table.
Keep the dog on leash.
Set your sight on the horizon.
His boss's pressure build
He pulled a gun on a suspect.
The student attends the college on a scholarship.
The workers are on strike.
The kid walks on bare foot.

〈under〉
They had Under impression
The suspect is under investigation.
The patient is under medication.
The staff are under pressure to find the solution.

9. 욕- profenity + 거친 말

이 글은 월간지 Vanity Fair 2024 9월호 월간지에 실렸다.
"Ah Shit" says Steve, owner of L.A. Clipper.
"Trump allies urge him not to be a 'raging ass hole' at debate."이라고 Rolling Stone 2024. 6. 26일 일간지에 실렸다.
그래도 CBS, NBC, ABC, PBS TV에서 이런 거친 말 들어본 기억이 없다. 이 Vanity Fair, New Yorker, The Atlantic 월간지 읽어보면 종종 욕이 나온다.

오래 전 "Up Your Ass." 번역을 찾을 수 없어 미국 친구 부인인 한국여성(고졸)에게 물어보니 "엿 먹어."를 아직도 모르냐고 웃으며 답해 주었다.
우리 집 소라는 내가 stupid, dumb 단어를 써도 쓰지 말라고 한다.

촌 사람: Hill billy, Redneck, bumpkin.
남을 이용해 먹는 인간: Leach, vulture.
여성: broad, chick(계집애 정도)
인종: Honky : 백인, Chink: 동양인, 중국인. Jab: 일본인.
더러운 인간: Scumbag, sleazeball.
Wetbag: Mexican.
Dyke: Lesbian.
Faggot, Queer: homosexual.
Boobs, jug, tits: female breast.
Behind, rear end, fanny, ass: buttock.
Ass hole: detestable person.
Bimbo: an attractive but stupid young woman.
Bullshit: stupid or untrue talk
Crap: foolish language, cheap materials.
Jerk: obnoxious person.
Piss off: being annoyed.
Shit: 대변, rubbish, nonsense.
Slut: sexually promiscuous woman

또라이, 지랄, 재수없어, 미쳤니 같은 단어를 조심스럽게 써야 할 언어라고 충고하는 한 글을 읽었다. 성적으로 심한 단어와 인종차별적인 욕(Racial Slurs)은 다른 Site에서 찾아볼 수 있다.

10-1. 미국 내 식당

⟨식당 리뷰(Review by Micherin)⟩
⟨지역한국신문(Local Korean Newspapers)⟩
L.A, Las Vegas, Chicago, NYC.

Los Angeles

1. JumSim(점심) 육개장, 떡볶이. 206 S. Spring St.
2. 고바우: 한식. 698 S. Vermont.
3. 조선옥 갈비, 냉면. 3,300 W. Olympic Blvd.
4. King Chang (고깃집) $ 30~50
5. 전주 한일관. 3,450 w. 6th St.
6. 소반: 4,001 w. Olympic Blvd.
7. 나무 Korean Tapas & BBQ. 809 S. Ardmore.
8. 모란각: 냉면 9651. Garden Grove Blvd, Garden Grove.
9. Chicken Bann: 닭 dish.113E. 9th St.
10. Baroo: 한식(expensive, $110)

Sandwich: Corner Bakery(chain)
American: BJ's: Jambalaya, Beers(Brewhouse)
Mexican: Sharky (chain) Nacho
Japanes: Hibi
Boiling Crab: 태국음식(Dungeness Crab, King crab)

Las Vegas

French: Burgundy Bakery. Sandwich & Onion Soup, 4.2 / 5.
9449 W. Sahara Ave.
Cajun: The Legends. Jambalaya. 4.5 / 5.
3220 S. Durango.
Chinese: Xiao Long Dumplings. 4.2 / 5.
4275 Spring Mountain Rd.
Thai: Archi's: Pha Thai. 오징어 사라드. 4.0 / 5.
9449 W. Sahara Ave.

한국식당

Mr. Tofu: 4353 Spring Mountain.
Hobak: 5808 Spring Mountain. BBQ 고기.
탕탕탕: 6000 Spring Mountain.
** 관광객 상대라(?) 맛에 비해 가격이 높다.

Chicago Area

Chickin: Buffalo Joe. rating 4.3 / 5. spicy. 812 Clark St. Evanston, Ill.

Italian Beef

1. Johnnie's in Elmwood Park.
2. Al's(chain) 3420 N. Clark st.
    Italy: Maggiano(chain): 해물 스파게티, calamari. 516 N. Clark St. (or Old Orchard)

Thick Pan Pizza

Giordano'S(chain)
Gino's East. 4곳에 있음.

뉴욕 시

초당골(M-4.1) 만두, 보쌈. 두부 전문.
기사(Kisa) 식당: $ 32불: 제육볶음, 오징어 볶음.
한가위(M-2, 4.5) 부추전- $12, 두부찌개 9불,
김밥- $19. 두부 김치찌게- $18.

페스트라미 in NYC

1, Katz's Delicatessen.
2, Pastrami Queen. Review by Anthony B.
But, in a 2017 interview with Variety, Bourdain places

Pastrami Queen at the top of the list of his hometown favorites. The first thing I get when I'm back in New York is a pastrami sandwich. Pastrami Queen is a really good pastrami sandwich

〈Michelin 상 받은 한국식당 in NYC〉 2023

아래 식당 5개는 가격이 아주 high.
정식(Jungsik) $ 295. 40-26 Green point, Long Island
오이지: 17 W. 19th St, New York,
꼬치(Kochi). 652 Tenth AVe. NYC.
메주(Meju) tasting menu-$ 185. MM-5-28 49th Ave. Queens, NY.

부록-10-2. 미국 내 Chain 식당

Chain Restaurants in the USA

⟨2021~2022⟩
Sale $ – No.stores – rate

⟨햄버거⟩

McDonald	$ 23.2 billion	40,275	**3.6 / 5.
Burger King	$ 23.4 billion	19,247	**3.6 / 5
Wendy	$ 12.5 billion	6,949	chili–3.6 / 5
In & Out	$ 1.8 billion	400	** 3.7 / 5.

⟨샌드위치⟩

Subway	$ 16.0 billion	36,999	
Jimmy John's	$ 5.5 billion	2,754	
Panera Bread	$ 5.9 billion	?	
Corner Bakery	$ 451 billion	192.	**3.8/ 5

**많이 쓰는 고기 (pastrami, corned beef, reast beef, ham, turkey)

⟨닭요리⟩

KFC	$ 31.3 billion	2,693	
Chick – fil	$ 18.8 billion	2,700	
Popeyes	$ 5.5 billion	3,750	3.5 / 5.
Buffalo Wild Wings	$ 3.67 billion	―xxx	

⟨Steak⟩

Texas RoadHouse	$ 3.0 billion	553	
Outback	$ 2.6 billion	724	3.6 / 5
LongHorn	$ 1.8 billion	530	

〈Regular〉 serving by employees.

Arby's	$ 3.8 billion	3,472	3.5 / 5.
Jack in the Box	$ 3.5 billion	2,267	
Applebee's	$ 4.2 billion	1,680	
BJ'S	$ 1.6 billion	215	**3.6 / 5
CheeseCake Factory	$ 2.16 billion	215	3.4/ 5

〈이태리 음식〉

Olive Garden	$ 4.02	919	
Maggiano's		52.***	3.8 / 5

〈피자〉

Pizza Hut	$ 17.7 billion	18,848	3.5 / 5.
Domino	$ 12.9 billion	18,381	
Little Caesars	$ 3.7 billion	5,460	
Papa John's	$ 2.0 billion	5,650	**3.6 / 5

〈멕시코〉

Taco Bell	$ 13.2 billion	7,791	
Chipotle	$ 5.5 billion	2,962	
Shakey's	XXXXX billion	−500+	** rate−3.6 / 5.

〈중국식당〉

Panda Express	$ 3.95 billion	USA−1,900	3.4 / 5.
Canada, Mexico, Korea, Saudi Arabia.	$ 5.5 billion	2,962	
P. F. Chang	$ XXXX billion	300	no rating